Microsoft® PowerPoint® 2003

Top 100
2nd Edition

Simplified®

TIPS & TRICKS

by Nancy Buchanan

Visual

WILEY

PowerPoint® 2003: Top 100 Simplified® Tips & Tricks, 2nd Edition

Published by
Wiley Publishing, Inc.
111 River Street
Hoboken, NJ 07030-5774

Published simultaneously in Canada

Copyright © 2005 by Wiley Publishing, Inc., Indianapolis, Indiana

Library of Congress Control Number: 2005923192

ISBN-13: 978-0-7645-9782-4

ISBN-10: 0-7645-9782-5

Manufactured in the United States of America

10 9 8 7 6 5 4 3 2 1

2K/QS/QW/QV/IN

Trademark Acknowledgments

Contact Us

For general information on our other products and services contact our Customer Care Department within the U.S. at 800-762-2974, outside the U.S. at 317-572-3993 or fax 317-572-4002.

For technical support please visit www.wiley.com/techsupport.

WILEY

Wiley Publishing, Inc.

Sales

Contact Wiley at (800) 762-2974 or fax (317) 572-4002.

PRAISE FOR VISUAL BOOKS

"I have to praise you and your company on the fine products you turn out. I have twelve Visual books in my house. They were instrumental in helping me pass a difficult computer course. Thank you for creating books that are easy to follow. Keep turning out those quality books."
Gordon Justin (Brielle, NJ)

"What fantastic teaching books you have produced! Congratulations to you and your staff. You deserve the Nobel prize in Education. Thanks for helping me understand computers."
Bruno Tonon (Melbourne, Australia)

"A Picture Is Worth A Thousand Words! If your learning method is by observing or hands-on training, this is the book for you!"
Lorri Pegan-Durastante (Wickliffe, OH)

"Over time, I have bought a number of your 'Read Less - Learn More' books. For me, they are THE way to learn anything easily. I learn easiest using your method of teaching."
José A. Mazón (Cuba, NY)

"You've got a fan for life!! Thanks so much!!"
Kevin P. Quinn (Oakland, CA)

"I have several books from the Visual series and have always found them to be valuable resources."
Stephen P. Miller (Ballston Spa, NY)

"I have several of your Visual books and they are the best I have ever used."
Stanley Clark (Crawfordville, FL)

"Like a lot of other people, I understand things best when I see them visually. Your books really make learning easy and life more fun."
John T. Frey (Cadillac, MI)

"I have quite a few of your Visual books and have been very pleased with all of them. I love the way the lessons are presented!"
Mary Jane Newman (Yorba Linda, CA)

"Thank you, thank you, thank you...for making it so easy for me to break into this high-tech world."
Gay O'Donnell (Calgary, Alberta,Canada)

"I write to extend my thanks and appreciation for your books. They are clear, easy to follow, and straight to the point. Keep up the good work! I bought several of your books and they are just right! No regrets! I will always buy your books because they are the best."
Seward Kollie (Dakar, Senegal)

"I would like to take this time to thank you and your company for producing great and easy-to-learn products. I bought two of your books from a local bookstore, and it was the best investment I've ever made! Thank you for thinking of us ordinary people."
Jeff Eastman (West Des Moines, IA)

"Compliments to the chef!! Your books are extraordinary! Or, simply put, extra-ordinary, meaning way above the rest! THANKYOU THANKYOU THANKYOU! I buy them for friends, family, and colleagues."
Christine J. Manfrin (Castle Rock, CO)

CREDITS

Project Editor
Jade L. Williams

Acquisitions Editor
Jody Lefevere

Product Development Manager
Lindsay Sandman

Copy Editor
Kim Heusel

Technical Editor
Allen Wyatt

Editorial Manager
Robyn Siesky

Manufacturing
Allan Conley
Linda Cook
Paul Gilchrist
Jennifer Guynn

Screen Artist
Elizabeth Cardenas-Nelson

Illustrator
Ronda David-Burroughs

Book Design
Kathryn S. Rickard

Production Coordinator
Maridee Ennis

Layout
Jennifer Heleine
Amanda Spagnuolo

Cover Design
Anthony Bunyan

Proofreader
Vicki Broyles

Quality Control
John Greenough
Susan Moritz

Special Help
Cara Buitron

Vice President and Executive Group Publisher
Richard Swadley

Vice President and Publisher
Barry Pruett

Composition Director
Debbie Stailey

ABOUT THE AUTHOR

Nancy Buchanan is a freelance high-tech marketing consultant and writer who has been in technical marketing and sales for more than 20 years. She was in product marketing for almost eight years at Microsoft Corporation, where she was a product manager for Microsoft Office, for Microsoft FrontPage, and for Windows-based streaming media. She was also responsible for marketing Microsoft products sold to attorneys. Prior to joining Microsoft, Nancy was in sales and marketing for over six years at Novell, inc. Nancy holds a bachelor of arts degree in business administration from University of Washington in Seattle and lives in Washington state with her husband, Doug, and her four children ranging in age from 5 to 15.

HOW TO USE THIS BOOK

PowerPoint® 2003: Top 100 Simplified® Tips & Tricks, 2nd Edition includes 100 tasks that reveal cool secrets, teach timesaving tricks, and explain great tips guaranteed to make you more productive with PowerPoint 2003. The easy-to-use layout lets you work through all the tasks from beginning to end or jump in at random.

Who is this book for?

You already know PowerPoint basics. Now you'd like to go beyond, with shortcuts, tricks and tips that let you work smarter and faster. And because you learn more easily when someone *shows* you how, this is the book for you.

Conventions Used In This Book

① Steps

This book uses step-by-step instructions to guide you easily through each task. Numbered callouts on every screen shot show you exactly how to perform each task, step by step.

② Tips

Practical tips provide insights to save you time and trouble, caution you about hazards to avoid, and reveal how to do things in PowerPoint 2003 that you never thought possible!

③ Task Numbers

Task numbers from 1 to 100 indicate which lesson you are working on.

④ Difficulty Levels

For quick reference, the symbols below mark the difficulty level of each task.

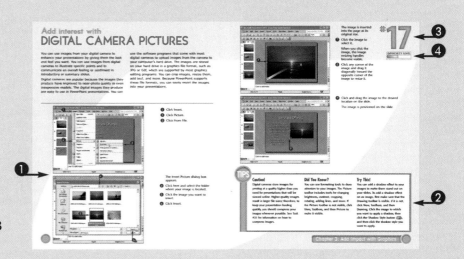

DIFFICULTY LEVEL	Demonstrates a new spin on a common task
DIFFICULTY LEVEL	Introduces a new skill or a new task
DIFFICULTY LEVEL	Combines multiple skills requiring in-depth knowledge
DIFFICULTY LEVEL	Requires extensive skill and may involve other technologies

Table of Contents

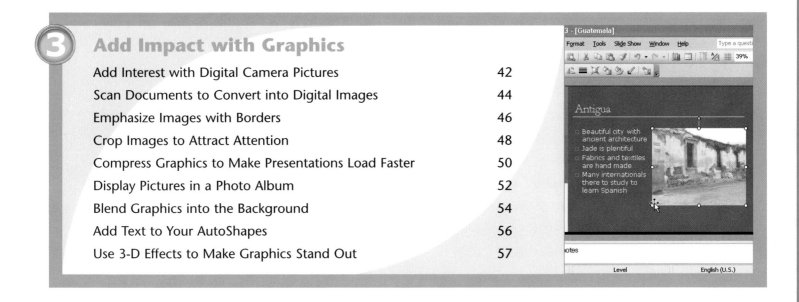

Add Impact with Graphics

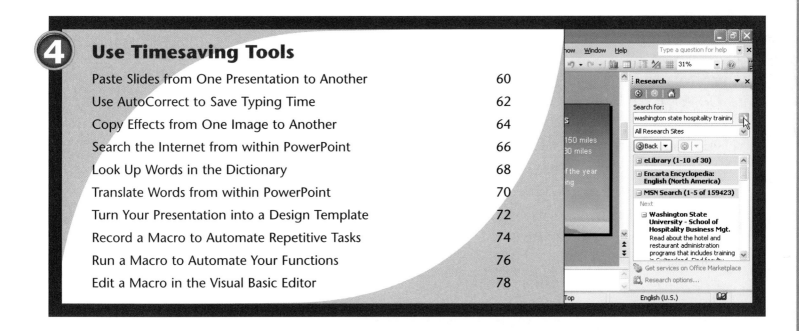

Use Timesaving Tools

Table of Contents

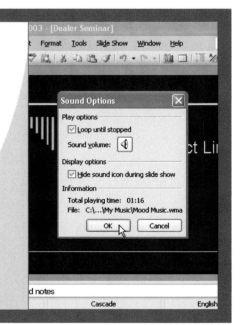

7 Enhance Your Presentations with Custom Content

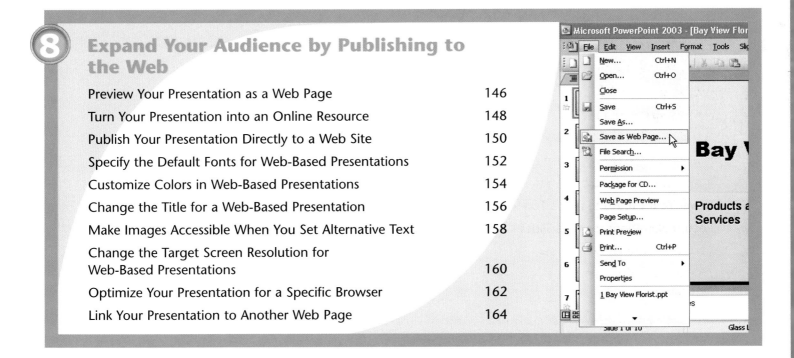

8 Expand Your Audience by Publishing to the Web

Table of Contents

Deliver and Distribute Your Presentation Effectively

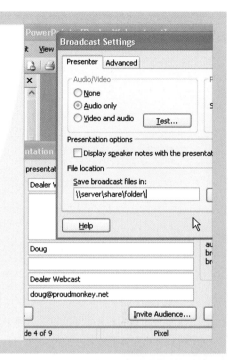

Customize PowerPoint Options to Suit Your Needs

You can get more done faster with PowerPoint 2003 when you customize its options to suit your needs. The tasks in this chapter are geared toward making the PowerPoint user interface work for you by helping you to place the tools you need where you need them.

If you have ever wondered how to open presentations with the Outline tab showing or with the Notes Page hidden, find out how here. It only takes a few minutes to configure PowerPoint to open presentations in the view in which you are most comfortable.

If you are tired of browsing to file folders many levels deep to find or save files, you can save time by adding a shortcut to the My Places Bar. You can customize menu

options so you can place the functions you use most where they work best for you. You can also create and name custom menus and toolbars according to your needs. Custom menus and toolbars can include virtually any function that is available in PowerPoint.

If you want to keep your PowerPoint working environment uncluttered and display only the functions you use most, you can choose which toolbars appear when you open PowerPoint. You can also choose whether or not the Office Clipboard opens every time you copy data to it so that you can easily access copied or pasted items, or instead concentrate on your presentation by choosing not to view Clipboard contents automatically.

Top 100

CHANGE THE VIEW
of your presentation

You can view presentations in the format in which you are most comfortable when you change the default view in which presentations display. For example, you may find that you routinely switch from the Slide tab to the Outline tab to see the organization of your presentation at a glance. On the other hand, you may find that you rarely use Notes, so you often turn off the Notes Page in order to concentrate on arranging your slides.

If you routinely change the way you view presentations in PowerPoint, you can save time

by specifying the default view you would like PowerPoint to use instead of making manual changes to the view each time you open a presentation. When you change the default view, PowerPoint displays only the parts of the screen that you want to see, such as the Outline or Slide tab, the Notes Page, or any combination of these options. After you specify the view you would like to use, you can see it take effect the next time you open a presentation.

① Click Tools.

② Click Options.

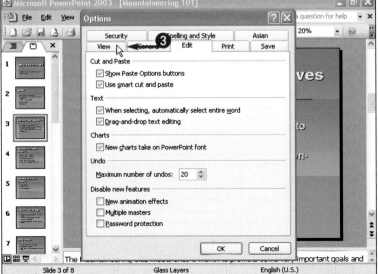

The Options dialog box opens.

③ Click the View tab.

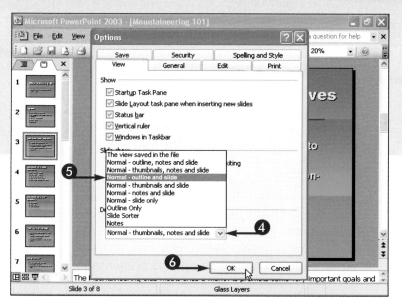

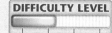
DIFFICULTY LEVEL

④ Click the Default View ☑.

⑤ Click a view option.

⑥ Click OK.

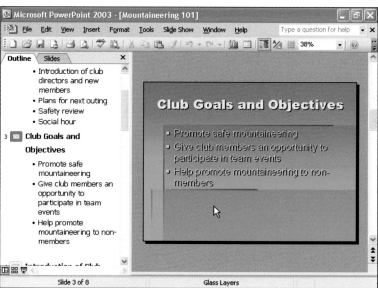

The Options dialog box closes, and the next time a presentation is opened, the view is changed.

TIPS

Did You Know?
You can always change a presentation's view after you open it. To view or remove the Notes Page, simply click View, and then click Notes Page.

Try This!
If you spend a lot of time reviewing presentations, you may want to set the default view to open presentations to the Slide Sorter. To do this, perform steps **1** to **4** above and then click the Slide Sorter option from the drop-down menu.

Customize It!
You can open presentations in the view in which the file was saved. To do this, perform steps **1** to **4** above, and then click the view saved in the file option from the drop-down menu.

ADD A SHORTCUT
to the My Places Bar

You can save time and access files quickly by adding a shortcut for commonly used folders to the My Places Bar. The My Places Bar appears on the Open and Save As dialog boxes and is most commonly used to access your Desktop, My Documents, My Computer, and My Network Places folders.

When you add a shortcut to the My Places Bar, it adds an icon to the bar that represents a file folder, network location, or even a Web site. When you want to open a file from that location, you can simply click

the shortcut to see the list of files that are available. Similarly, when you save a file, you can click the shortcut to save files directly to that location. You are also able to continue to browse folders even after you click the shortcut; shortcuts in the My Places Bar are often used to quickly get to a hard drive or network drive and then locate the specific folder you want to use thereafter.

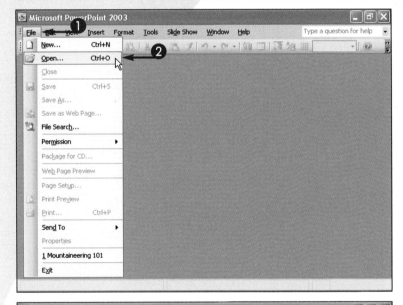

ADD THE SHORTCUT

1. Click File.

2. Click Open.

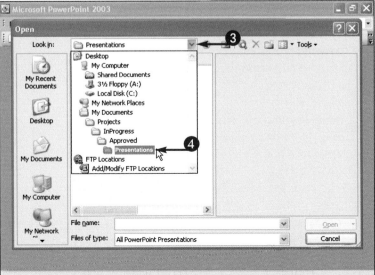

The Open dialog box appears.

3. Click the Look in ⊡.

4. Click a folder location.

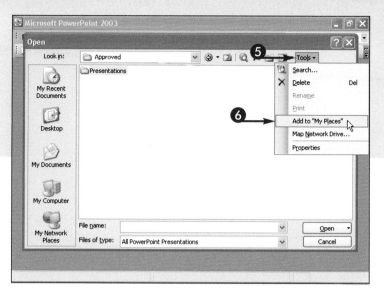

5 Click the Tools ⬇.

6 Click Add to "My Places".

The shortcut is added to the My Places Bar.

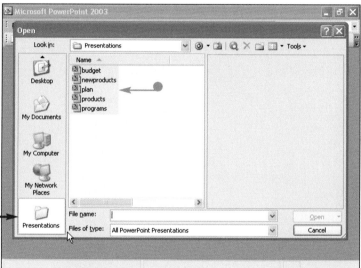

USE THE SHORTCUT

1 In the Open or Save As dialog box, click the shortcut icon on the My Places Bar.

● The folder opens.

TIPS

Did You Know?

Because all of the Microsoft Office 2003 programs use the My Places Bar, when you add a shortcut to your My Places Bar in PowerPoint, it is also accessible in other programs like Microsoft Word, Microsoft Excel, and more.

Attention!

If you add a shortcut to a password-protected network location or Web site, a prompt may appear asking for a valid user name and password before you can access the shortcut location.

Use the Web!

You can also add Web site shortcuts to My Network Places instead of creating shortcuts on the My Places Bar. You can add My Network Places by clicking Start, My Network Places, and then Add a network place.

Customize
MENU OPTIONS

You can put the features you use within easy access by customizing menu bar options in PowerPoint 2003. Menus, such as File, Edit, View, and Insert, make it fast and easy to access PowerPoint tools.

You can easily add commands to menus or remove menu items that you do not need or use. You can move menu items that are currently nested in submenus to a place of higher prominence on the menu, or you can easily rearrange menu items to put the tools you need where you need them.

For example, if you work with many files, you may frequently use the File Search command. The File Search command is not listed on any of the default menus. However, you can add this command to any of the menus to make this tool easy to access.

More advanced options allow you to change or add an icon next to a menu item, change the text label for a menu item, or even change the shortcut key for a menu item.

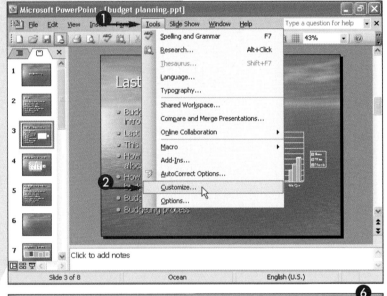

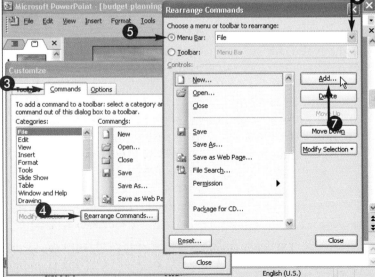

① Click Tools.

② Click Customize.

The Customize dialog box appears.

③ Click the Commands tab to customize your menus.

④ Click the Rearrange Commands button.

The Rearrange Commands dialog box appears.

⑤ Click the Menu Bar option (○ changes to ◉).

⑥ Click here and select a menu to edit.

⑦ Click Add.

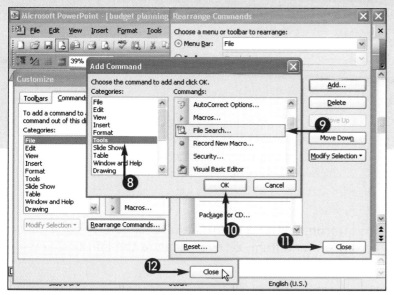

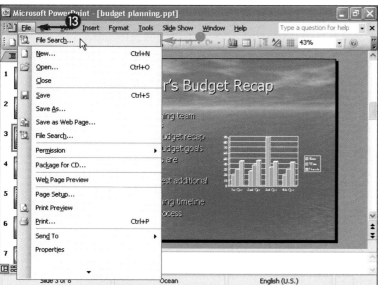

The Add Command dialog box appears.

⑧ In the Categories section, click a menu from which you want to select a command.

⑨ In the Commands section, scroll down and click a command to add to the menu.

⑩ Click OK.

The menu is updated.

⑪ Click Close to close the Rearrange Commands dialog box.

⑫ Click Close to close the Customize dialog box.

The new command is added to the menu.

⑬ Click the menu to which you added a new command.

● The command is now visible on the menu.

TIPS

Move It!
You can easily change the order of commands on menus. Follow steps **1** to **6** above. In the Controls section, scroll down and click the command you want to move, and then click the Move Up or Move Down button.

Try This!
You can also change the text label on menu items. To modify menu text, follow steps **1** to **6** above, and then click the Modify Selection button. The menu that appears gives you options for renaming menu item labels and more.

Reset It!
If you are unhappy with changes you have made to a menu, you can reset the menu to its original state. Simply follow steps **1** to **6** above, and then click the Reset button at the bottom of the Rearrange Commands dialog box.

Create a
NEW MENU

You can create your own menus to put all of the commands and tools that you need for a specific type of presentation or for all presentations in one familiar place. You can access your custom menus along with the other standard menus like the File, Edit, View, Insert, Format, and Tools menus by clicking them on the menu in PowerPoint. You can choose where to position your custom menu relative to the other menus to customize the PowerPoint environment even further.

Custom menus work well when you need to access tools that are normally found on different menus from the one you are using. For example, if you routinely work on presentations that require frequent edits to tables, additions of hyperlinks, and formatting of bulleted lists, you can easily set up a custom menu with a name you choose that you can use to link to these tools. Without a custom menu, you would have had to open three different menus to gain access to these tools.

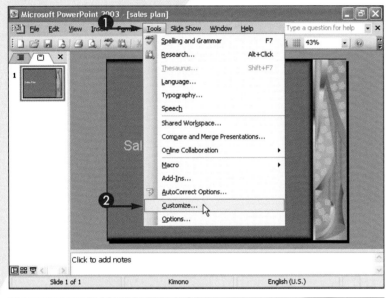

① Click Tools.

② Click Customize.

The Customize dialog box appears.

③ Click the Commands tab.

④ In the Categories section, scroll down and click New Menu.

⑤ Click and drag New Menu from the Commands scroll box to the position you desire on the menu.

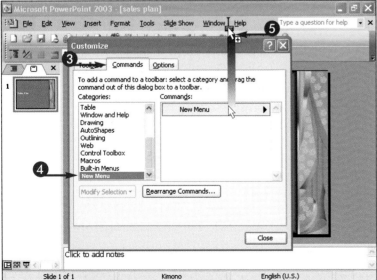

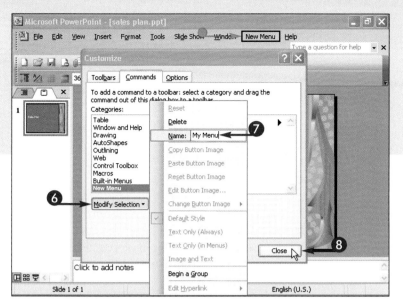

- The New Menu item appears on the menu.

6 Click Modify Selection.

The Modify Selection menu appears.

7 Type a name for your menu in the Name field and then press Enter.

8 Click Close.

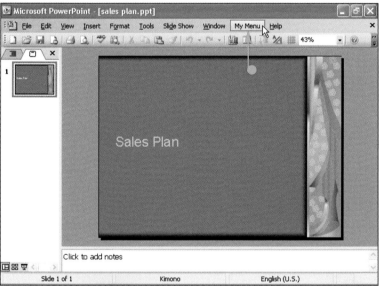

- The modified menu name appears on the menu.

Note: For more information about customizing menu items, see Task #3.

TIPS

Did You Know?

You can specify the shortcut key used to access a menu or menu item. Follow steps **1** to **7** above, but type an ampersand (&) before the letter you wish to use as the shortcut key in the Name box. For example, to make your custom menu named My Menu accessible when you press Alt+U, type **My Men&u** in the Name field. The menu will then appear as My Men<u>u</u>.

Delete It!

You can easily delete a menu. Follow steps **1** to **5** and then click Rearrange Commands. Click the Toolbar option to select it, click the Toolbar down arrow, and then click a menu to edit. Click Delete and then Close.

CHANGE THE TOOLBARS
on display

You can easily get to the tools you need by specifying which toolbars to display and which toolbars to hide by default when you open PowerPoint. Toolbars make it easy to find similar tools in one place, and unlike menus, which you click and then they expand to display options, toolbars display their contents in the user interface, making their features even faster to access. Unlike menus, you can reposition toolbars on the presentation on which you are working. You can also resize toolbars to expose all or only a few of the buttons contained in them.

PowerPoint comes with a variety of toolbars, including the Standard, Formatting, Drawing, Picture, and E-mail toolbars and more. Toolbars take up screen space that you can use for editing your presentation; therefore, be selective about which toolbars you display. For example, if you routinely spend a lot of time working on graphics, you may want to make sure that only the Standard, Formatting, Drawing, and Picture toolbars are open.

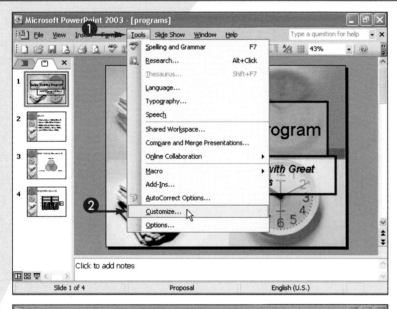

① Click Tools.

② Click Customize.

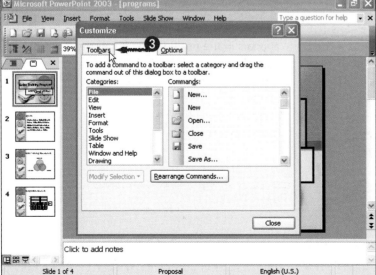

The Customize dialog box opens.

③ Click the Toolbars tab.

4 In the Toolbars list, click the toolbars that you want to display (☐ changes to ☑).

5 Click Close.

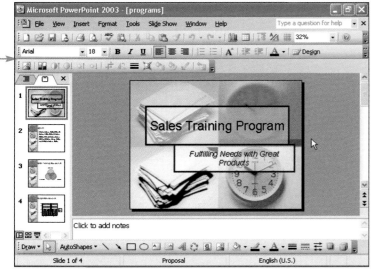

● The toolbars you selected appear.

TIPS

Move It!
Each toolbar has four vertical dots (⁞) that help you move toolbars to a fixed position on the screen, such as any of the margins of the screen, or to floating positions on the screen where you can place them on top of the work area. To position a toolbar, click ⁞ on the toolbar that you want to move and then drag it to the desired position.

Did You Know?
When you choose to view a toolbar, it appears in the position that it was most recently used, such as docked in a menu or floating in the presentation window. You may need to move toolbars around to find the position that is right for you.

Turn on and off the
OFFICE CLIPBOARD

The Office Clipboard automatically saves up to 24 pieces of data that you copy. The Office Clipboard is a Microsoft Office resource that you can use across all Microsoft Office programs, including PowerPoint. The Office Clipboard provides a visual representation of the items stored, which makes it easier to collect information from a variety of sources and then selectively paste it into your presentation when you are ready. Data is automatically stored to the Office Clipboard when you copy data in Microsoft Office programs and Internet Explorer.

The Office Clipboard is accessible from the Clipboard Task Pane in PowerPoint. The Clipboard Task Pane is convenient to use when you are collecting data to paste into a presentation. However, if you commonly copy and then paste data but do not need to save it for reuse, you may want to turn off the automatic display of the Office Clipboard to save desktop space when you are working on a presentation. You can also stop collecting data on the Office Clipboard.

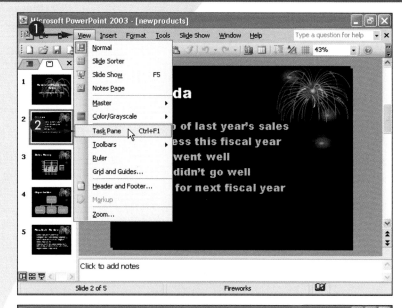

① Click View.

② Click Task Pane.

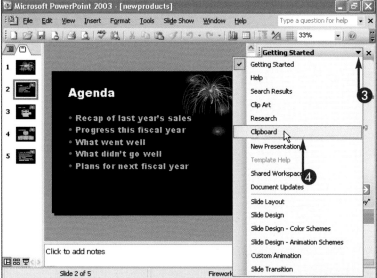

The Task Pane opens.

③ Click the Task Pane ▾.

④ Click Clipboard.

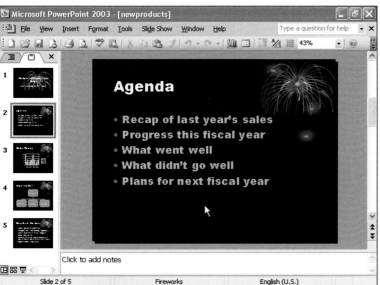

The Clipboard Task Pane appears.

⑤ Click Options.

⑥ Click to uncheck the Show Office Clipboard Automatically option (☑ changes to ☐).

⑦ Click the Show Office Clipboard When Ctrl+C Pressed Twice option (☐ changes to ☑).

⑧ Click to uncheck the Collect Without Showing Office Clipboard option (☑ changes to ☐).

⑨ Click ☒ to close the Clipboard Task Pane.

The Clipboard Task Pane closes.

The Clipboard still collects data, but the Clipboard does not open when new items are collected.

TIPS

Try This!

If you are copying large amounts of data, such as large graphics files, they will stay on the Office Clipboard and in your computer's memory until you exit from all Office programs. To clear the Office Clipboard, follow steps **1** to **4** above, and then click the Clear All button on the Clipboard Task Pane.

Stop It!

You can choose to stop collecting data in the Office Clipboard altogether. Follow steps **1** to **5** above, and then clear the check boxes (☐) next to the Show Office Clipboard Automatically, Collect Without Showing Office Clipboard, and Show Office Clipboard When Ctrl+C Pressed Twice options (☑ changes to ☐). Click ☒ to close the Clipboard Task Pane.

Chapter 2

Give Your Presentation the Look You Want

You can use tools in PowerPoint 2003 to give your presentations a professional look that gets your work noticed. If you have ever wanted an easy way to check to see if your presentation meets visual goals, the Style Checker and the Office Assistant together can help. They can save you time by informing you when slides are becoming too cluttered or when too many fonts are being used. They can even suggest and then implement improvements for you.

You can also give your presentations a consistent format across presentations by using Slide Masters. You can create your own Slide Masters to suit your unique formatting needs.

You can emphasize a key message or logo when you place watermark text or a watermark image in the background of a printed slide.

You can also place slide numbers on each slide in a presentation to make it easier for audience members to find particular slides.

If you are looking for ways to provide consistency across presentations, printed materials, and Web sites, you can find out how to change the fonts used throughout an entire presentation. You can use custom graphics or other materials from a Web site as bullets in your presentations or background images for slides. You can also quickly change the layout of slides whenever needed.

If you work with international customers, partners, or coworkers, you can enable the display and editing of content in a wide variety of languages to expand the impact of your presentation.

Top 100

Set Visual Clarity Rules to define your
FORMATTING RULES

You can make your presentations easy for audience members to read and follow by setting Visual Clarity Rules and then setting alerts to warn you when slides do not meet those rules. Most instructors who teach presentation skills recommend guidelines for maintaining visual clarity, such as using font sizes that are large enough to be legible, limiting the number of bullets per slide, and limiting the number of lines per bullet.

You can use PowerPoint's Visual Clarity Rules to specify your own thresholds for font size, the number of bullets per slide, and the number of lines per bullet. Once these Visual Clarity goals are set, the Visual Clarity checker uses the Office Assistant to let you know when goals are not being met.

When the Office Assistant finds an issue on a slide, a subtle light bulb icon is placed on the slide. You can click the light bulb icon to find out more about the issue and then act upon suggestions for improvement.

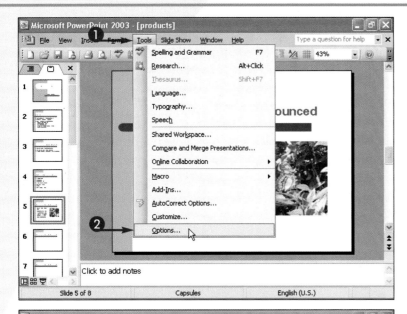

❶ Click Tools.

❷ Click Options.

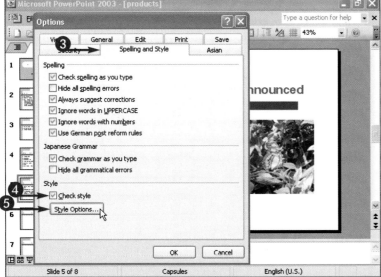

The Options dialog box appears.

❸ Click the Spelling and Style tab.

❹ Click the Check style option (☐ changes to ☑).

If you do not have the Office Assistant enabled, a dialog box opens to prompt you to do so.

❺ Click Style Options.

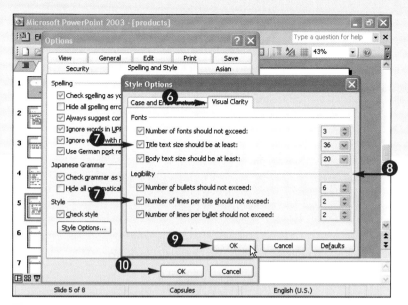

The Style Options dialog box appears.

6 Click the Visual Clarity tab.

7 In the Fonts section, click the Visual Clarity options you want to enforce.

8 Click here to specify the Visual Clarity settings you want for the items you checked in step **7**.

9 Click OK.

10 Click OK in the Options dialog box.

The Options dialog box closes.

The Office Assistant places a light bulb icon on each page that violates the Visual Clarity Rules you set.

11 Click each light bulb icon.

The Office Assistant suggests ways to change the presentation.

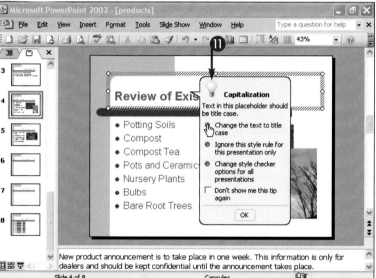

Attention!

You can see if the Office Assistant has been enabled on your computer by clicking Help and then clicking Show the Office Assistant. If it has not been installed, you are prompted to install it. You may have to go into the PowerPoint installation program to install the Office Assistant.

Did You Know?

If you do not want to be reminded of Visual Clarity violations all the time, uncheck the Check style option in step **4** (☑ changes to ☐). When you are once again ready for compliance reminders, click the Check style option in step **4** (☐ changes to ☑).

Change layouts when you
CREATE YOUR OWN MASTERS

You can change the look of all of the slides in your presentation when you create a new Slide Master. Slide Masters are templates that define how slides are formatted. Slide Masters also allow you to insert common elements on every slide, such as slide number, the date, footer text, or even logos or pictures. If you want all of the slides in your presentation to use similar fonts, formatting, and graphics, Slide Masters are the best way to do this.

You may want to create a new Slide Master instead of editing the existing one if you want to apply it only

to selected slides or if you only plan to use it for a short time. You may also want to create a new Slide Master, and then apply it to the main Slide Master once you are sure how you want it. This task explains how to create a new Slide Master from an existing one, and then apply it to a slide or a presentation.

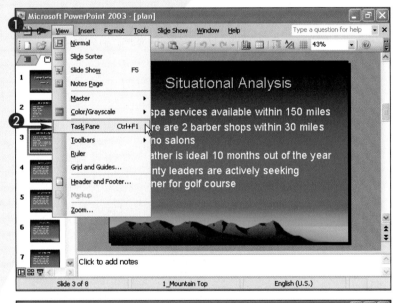

❶ Click View.

❷ Click Task Pane.

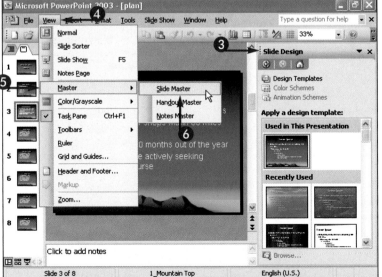

The Task Pane appears.

❸ Click here and select Slide Design.

The Slide Design Task Pane appears.

❹ Click View.

❺ Click Master.

❻ Click Slide Master.

8

DIFFICULTY LEVEL

The Slide Master View toolbar and the list of Slide and Title Masters appear.

⑦ Click Insert.

⑧ Click Duplicate Slide Master.

● The Slide Master and Title Master are duplicated. The new Slide Master appears in the Slide Design Task Pane.

⑨ Edit the new Slide Master as desired.

⑩ Click Close Master View.

The Normal View of your presentation appears.

⑪ Click the ▮ next to the new Slide Master.

⑫ Click Apply to Selected Slides.

The new Slide Master is applied to your slide.

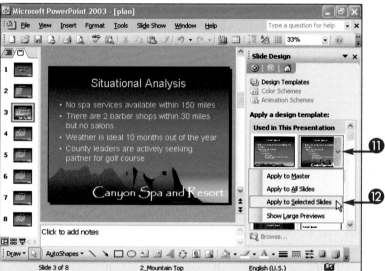

TIPS

Apply It!
You can apply the new Slide Master to all of the slides in your presentation. Follow steps **1** to **11** above, and then click Apply to All Slides.

Did You Know?
You can make your new Slide Master the main Slide Master. Follow steps **1** to **11** above, and then click Apply to Master.

Name It!
You can change the name of the new Slide Master by following steps **1** to **10** above, and then clicking the Rename Master button (🔲) on the Slide Master View toolbar.

Did You Know?
You can start with a blank Slide Master by following steps **1** to **7** above. On step **8**, click New Slide Master instead of Duplicate Slide Master.

ADD A WATERMARK
to your slides

You can communicate an important message or display a key image behind the text when you add watermarks to your presentations. Watermarks are commonly used to identify documents as a *draft*, as *confidential*, or with other messages. You can use watermarks to reinforce branding and corporate images by placing logos or marketing taglines behind text. Watermarks are most effective when they communicate the intended message without interfering with the slide. This is usually accomplished by using subtle colors that maintain the legibility of slide content.

Watermarks are different from the graphics you insert into your presentation because the watermarks print behind your Notes or Handout pages. They also print on every page because they are placed on Notes or Handout Masters that duplicate the text or images to all of the pages.

You can easily create attention-getting watermarks by using the tools available in the Drawing Toolbar. You can create AutoShapes like callouts, stars, and banners, and insert text in them to deliver your messages. You can also insert WordArt and diagram objects that you can rotate or reformat however you choose.

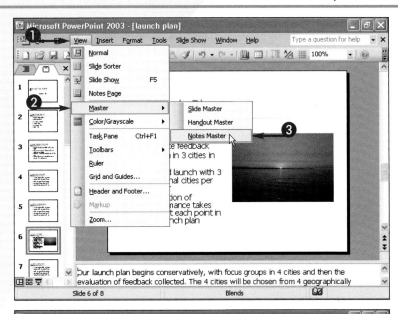

❶ Click View.

❷ Click Master.

❸ Click Notes Master.

The Notes Master appears.

❹ Click View.

❺ Click Toolbars.

❻ Click Drawing.

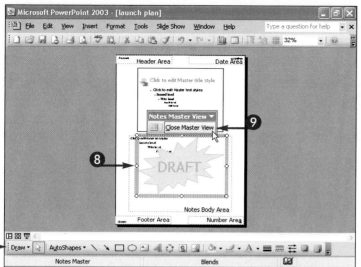

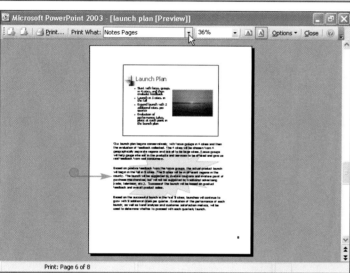

Print: Page 6 of 8

The Drawing toolbar appears.

7 Click to select a tool from the Drawing toolbar.

8 Click in the presentation and add a text box, an AutoShape, or a picture as your watermark.

9 Click Close Master View.

The Notes Master closes.

● When the Notes Page is printed, the watermark appears behind the text.

 # 9

DIFFICULTY LEVEL

TIPS

Did You Know?
You can also create watermarks behind Handout pages. Follow steps **1** and **2** above, and then click Handout Master instead of Notes Master.

Did You Know?
You can use Print Preview to see how your watermarks will look when printed. You can access Print Preview by clicking File and then Print Preview. It is a good idea to confirm how pages will print because pages with slides that cover the majority of the page will leave much of the watermark covered. Using Print Preview shows you what areas of the page are not covered by slides and display your watermark when printed.

PLACE SLIDE NUMBERS
on all slides

You can easily insert numbers on slides to make them easier for audience members to reference. You may already be accustomed to placing page numbers on Slide, Handout, and Notes pages so that anyone following a printed copy of your presentation can easily find referenced pages. However, inserting numbers on slides enables audience members to ask questions about specific slides regardless of whether the audience member is looking at a Handout page printed with six slides per page or a Notes page that includes only one slide per page. Similarly, if an

audience member wants to ask a question about a slide and there are multiple slides with similar titles, adding slide numbers makes it easier for a viewer to ask about a specific slide.

Slide numbers are included on Notes and Handout pages by default, but they are not turned on for slides by default. This task explains how to add numbers to all slides in a presentation, and then how to edit slide number formatting.

① Click Insert.

② Click Slide Number.

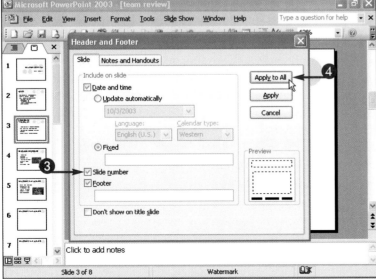

The Header and Footer dialog box appears.

③ Click the Slide number option (☐ changes to ☑).

④ Click Apply to All.

The Header and Footer dialog box closes.

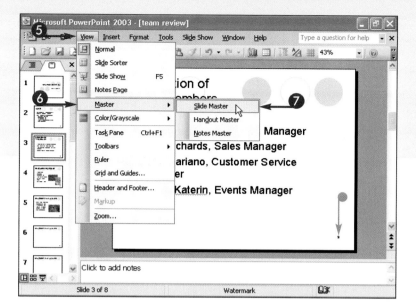

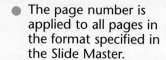

DIFFICULTY LEVEL

- The page number is applied to all pages in the format specified in the Slide Master.

⑤ Click View.

⑥ Click Master.

⑦ Click Slide Master.

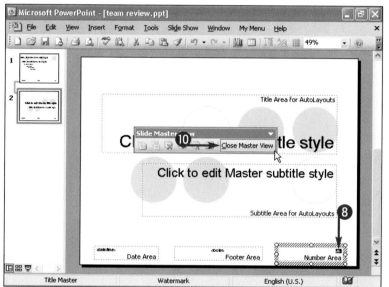

The Slide Master View appears.

⑧ Click to highlight the slide number symbol ( ).

⑨ Press Ctrl+B to change the font to bold.

You can also change the formatting of the slide number by clicking Format and selecting an option.

⑩ Click Close Master View.

Slide numbers are applied to all pages in the format specified.

TIPS

Did You Know?

When you add slide numbers to the slides in your presentation, they are also displayed when you print your slides.

Apply It!

After you insert numbers into your slides, view them in Slide Show Mode to make sure that they are clearly visible. You can access Slide Show Mode by clicking Slide Show and then View Show. You can use Print Preview to see how they will look when they are printed by clicking File and then Print Preview.

Did You Know?

You can easily insert slide numbers into individual slides instead of all slides. Follow steps **1** to **4** above, but instead of clicking Apply to All in step **4**, click Apply.

CHANGE THE FONTS
in your presentation

You can give your presentation a completely different look by changing the fonts used in your presentation. Font changes can transform a presentation from casual to professional to classic to formal.

Changing all fonts at one time can be especially useful when you have chosen to use a Design Template that has the look and feel you like, but uses a font that is different from what your company normally uses. Changing fonts can help ensure consistency with other materials you produce, such as written reports.

You can change fonts used throughout your presentation by changing the fonts in the Masters that control the formatting of your presentation. However, changing fonts in Slide Masters does not affect text in items not controlled by the Masters, such as text boxes. If you want to change fonts throughout your presentation, including in Masters, text boxes, and more, you can use Replace Fonts to replace one font with another. This task explains how selected fonts can be changed by using Replace Fonts to globally replace one font used in your presentation with another.

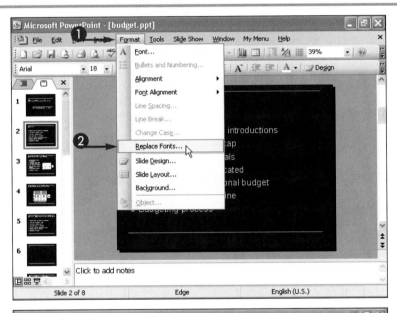

① Click Format.

② Click Replace Fonts.

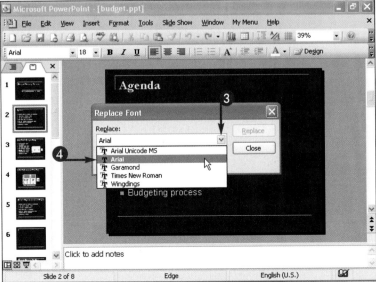

The Replace Font dialog box appears.

③ Click the Replace ▾.

④ Click the font you want to replace.

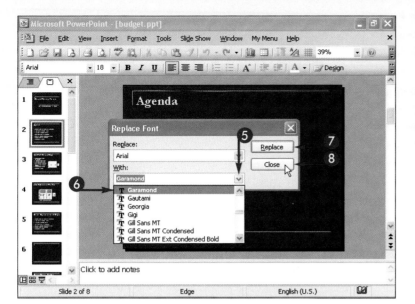

5 Click the With ⌄.

6 Click the font with which you want to replace the existing font.

7 Click Replace.

8 Click Close.

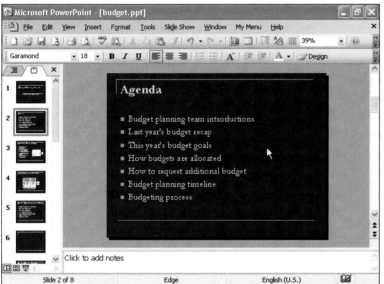

The font is replaced throughout the entire presentation.

TIPS

Caution!

Replace Fonts changes the font used everywhere in your presentation, including in Masters. Therefore, even if you select text that is 12-point Arial and use Replace Fonts to change it to Georgia, every instance of the Arial font will change to Georgia. Because the changes made with Replace Fonts are so global, use this tool with caution.

Did You Know?

If you want to change fonts on elements that are controlled by a Slide Master, but only want those changes to apply to specific slides, you can create a new Slide Master to apply to selected slides. See Task #8 for information about how to create a new Slide Master.

EMPHASIZE SLIDE TITLES
by changing their case

You can choose to emphasize slide titles by setting capitalization options for slide titles, such as sentence case, lowercase, uppercase, or title case. Sentence case capitalizes the first word of a line, lowercase uses all lowercase letters, uppercase capitalizes all letters, and title case capitalizes the first letter of each word.

You can use the Style Checker to set title capitalization rules, and you can choose to instruct the Office Assistant to alert you when a slide title

does not meet the capitalization rules you set. For example, if you choose to use uppercase slide titles, a slide that violates this rule would display a light bulb icon to remind you that there is an issue with the slide. When you click the icon you can change the slide title's capitalization to meet the rules you set, you can choose to go back into the Style Checker to change your formatting choices, or you can choose to ignore formatting rules for this presentation.

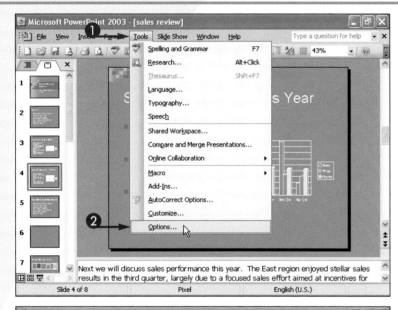

❶ Click Tools.

❷ Click Options.

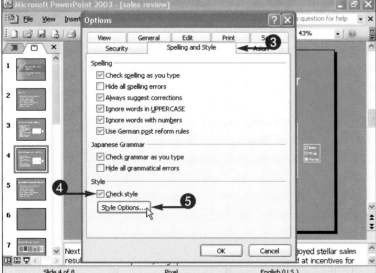

The Options dialog box appears.

❸ Click the Spelling and Style tab.

❹ Click the Check style option
(☐ changes to ☑).

If you do not have the Office Assistant enabled, a dialog box opens to prompt you to do so.

❺ Click Style Options.

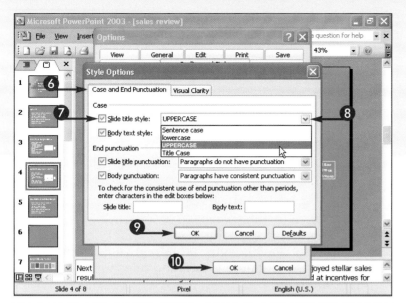

The Style Options dialog box appears.

6 Click the Case and End Punctuation tab.

7 Click the Slide title style option (☐ changes to ☑).

8 Click here and select UPPERCASE.

9 Click OK to close the Style Options dialog box.

10 Click OK to close the Options dialog box.

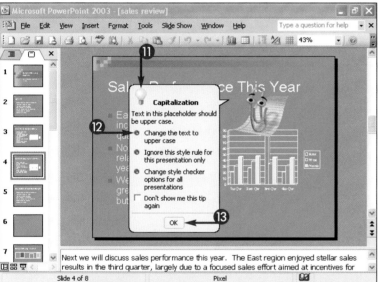

The Office Assistant places a light bulb icon on each page that does not use uppercase titles.

11 Click each light bulb icon.

The Office Assistant suggests changes to the presentation.

12 Click the Change the text to upper case option to change the slide's title to all capital letters.

13 Click OK.

The slide title is capitalized.

TIPS

Attention!

The Style Checker requires the Office Assistant. You can find out whether the Office Assistant has been enabled on your computer by clicking Help and then Show the Office Assistant. If it has not been installed, you are prompted to install it. You may have to go into the PowerPoint or Office installation program to install the Office Assistant.

Did You Know?

You can also use the Style Checker to define and then check for capitalization of body text. Follow steps **1** to **13** above, but in step **7**, click the Body text style option instead of Slide title style option (☐ changes to ☑).

CREATE UNIQUE POINTS
from your own custom graphics

You can give your presentations the look you want when you use your own custom graphics for bullets. Bullets are the graphical elements placed before text in most slides. Each level in most presentations uses different bullets, or different sized bullets. Therefore, you may want to import and then use various graphics files for each level of content in your presentation.

You can use custom bullets that you create with a graphics program or utilize the bullets that you use on your Web site in your presentations as well. Using

consistent graphics across all of the documents you create, as well as the presentations you produce, helps reinforce your company's brand and image with a unified look.

The graphics files from which you create bullets can be in any file format supported by PowerPoint, which includes virtually all of the most popular graphics files. Once you use a custom graphics file as a picture bullet, it continues to be accessible from the Picture Bullets library for other projects.

❶ Click and drag to select the text next to the bullets you want to change.

❷ Click Format.

❸ Click Bullets and Numbering.

The Bullets and Numbering dialog box appears.

❹ Click Picture.

The Picture Bullet dialog box appears.

❺ Click Import.

30

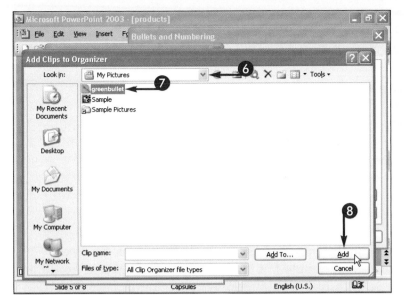

The Add Clips to Organizer dialog box appears.

6 Click here to locate the folder where your graphic files are stored.

7 Click the name of the graphic file you want to use in place of the current bullet.

8 Click Add.

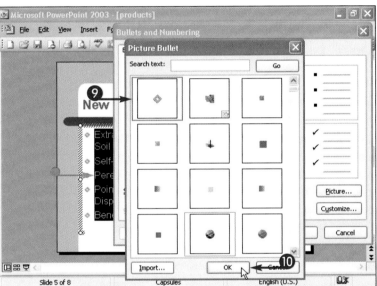

The Picture Bullet dialog box appears.

9 Click your custom bullet.

10 Click OK.

The Picture Bullet and Bullets and Numbering dialog boxes close.

● The presentation is updated with the new custom bullet.

Apply It!

You can easily change the bullets throughout your presentation by altering the bullets used in Slide Masters. To access Slide Masters, click View and then Slide Masters. Edit the bullets by following steps **1** to **10** above and then click Close Master View. All of the slides using that Master are updated with your custom bullets.

Did You Know?

You can run presentations faster when you make sure the graphics files that you use are not large. Instead of using bullets that are uncompressed, such as BMP or TIF files, try using smaller, compressed graphics formats, such as JPG or GIF files.

CHANGE THE LAYOUT
of an existing slide

You can freely change the layout of elements such as text, bulleted lists, graphics, buttons, animations, audio or video clips, and more on your slides whenever you want. You can easily click and drag elements to move them, or insert items like diagrams, graphs, and charts where needed. Better yet, you can save time when you use Slide Layouts to add elements and rearrange existing items without clicking and dragging and resizing elements on the slide.

The Slide Layout Task Pane gives you a clear visual representation of the many available layouts so you can quickly identify the right layout for your content. You can use the Slide Layout Task Pane to apply a layout to a selected slide or to a new slide. Once the layout has been applied to the slide, you can easily insert pictures, text, audio, video, and more, and that content is placed according to your Slide Layout choices. If your content dictates a change in layout, you can easily choose from one of the other layouts whenever you want.

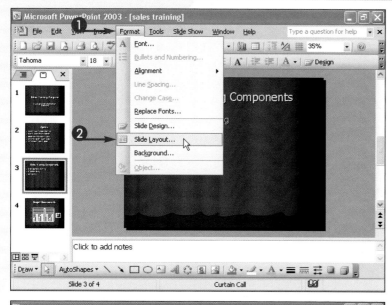

❶ Click Format.

❷ Click Slide Layout.

The Slide Layout Task Pane appears.

❸ In the Apply slide layout section, click the ▌ on the Slide Layout that you want to apply.

❹ Click Apply to Selected Slides.

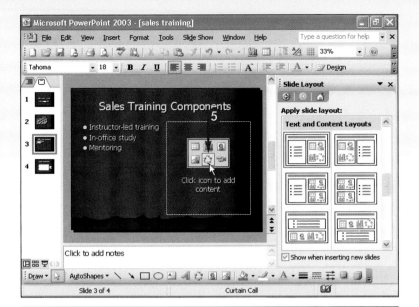

The new slide layout is applied.

5 Click one of the icons to insert a table, a chart, a picture, a diagram, or a video clip.

The appropriate dialog box opens, for example, the Diagram Gallery.

6 Click the item you want to insert into the slide.

7 Click OK.

The item is inserted into the slide in the specified slide layout.

TIPS

Apply It!
If the Slide Layout Task Pane is already visible and you want to create a new slide, follow steps **1** to **7**, but in step **4**, click Insert New Slide instead of Apply to Selected Slides.

Stop It!
The Slide Layout Task Pane opens when you create a new slide. If you do not want it to open automatically, follow steps **1** and **2** above, and then click to uncheck the Show when inserting new slides option (☑ changes to ☐).

Did You Know?
You can easily create slides with organizational charts, tables, graphs, audio and video clips, and more. Look for these options in the Apply Slide Layout section of the Slide Layouts Task Pane.

Add emphasis by inserting a
CUSTOM BACKGROUND IMAGE

You can create a professional-looking and fully customized presentation by inserting a unique or custom background image into a slide. The background image, which can come from a digital camera, from a drawing program, or from a professional graphics design, can greatly enhance the look of your presentation.

When you insert an image as a slide background, it does not print when the slides print. This is important, because if you apply a background image for its appearance, you do not want the image to conflict with the slide content. If you want the image to print with the slide, insert the image into the slide itself.

Background images are stretched or contracted to display on whatever screen that is being used. For example, if your image is very small, when the presentation is viewed in Slide Show Mode, it will automatically stretch to fit the screen. You will get better results if you use images that are approximately the same size as the monitor on which you will display them.

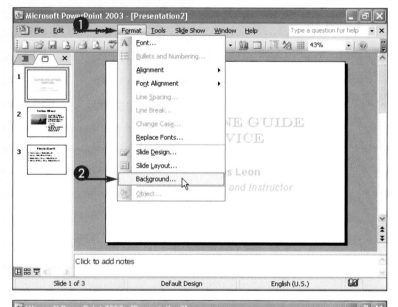

① Click Format.

② Click Background.

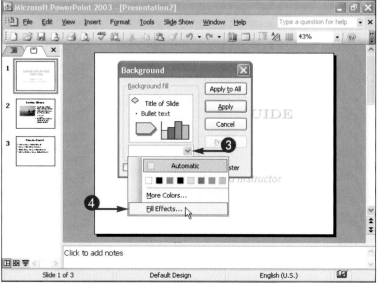

The Background dialog box appears.

③ Click the Colors ▾.

④ Click Fill Effects.

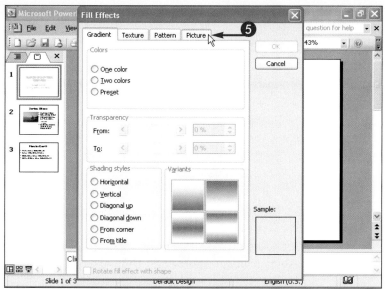

The Fill Effects dialog box appears.

⑤ Click the Picture tab.

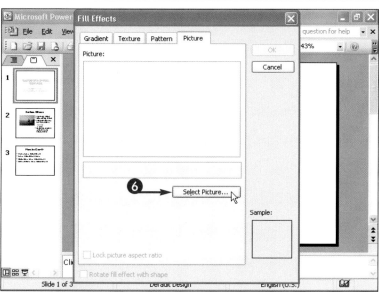

⑥ Click Select Picture.

Caution!

You will achieve the best results when you apply a background image that is 1⅓ times wider than it is high. The width of most computer screen resolutions is 1⅓ times the height, such as 800 pixels wide by 600 pixels high. Your background image should use these proportions as well. If the image you are using for a background is not in these proportions, the background image will look stretched or skewed when displayed.

Apply It!

You can also apply textures to slide backgrounds. To do so, follow steps **1** to **4** above, then click the Texture tab, click the texture you want to apply, and then click OK.

Add emphasis by inserting a
CUSTOM BACKGROUND IMAGE

Pictures from digital cameras work well as background images for slides. Because most newer digital cameras create images with higher resolutions than are needed for use in presentations, you may want to reduce the size of the file in a graphics editing program before you use it for a background image.

In addition to images taken from a digital camera, you can use graphics files in any picture file format supported by Microsoft Office, including BMP, JPG, GIF, TIF, and more. Remember that if you use uncompressed files or files that are larger than

needed, you may unnecessarily increase the file size of your presentation or even slow its performance when delivering a slide show.

The best images to use for slide backgrounds are relatively uniform in color in the areas that contain text. For example, an image that is very light on one half and very dark on the other half would not work well as a background image because it is extremely difficult, if not impossible, to find a font and font color combination that work well against both light and dark backgrounds.

The Select Picture dialog box appears.

7 Click here and locate the folder containing the file you want to use as the background image.

8 Click the file you want to use.

9 Click Insert.

The Fill Effects dialog box reappears displaying the image.

10 Click OK.

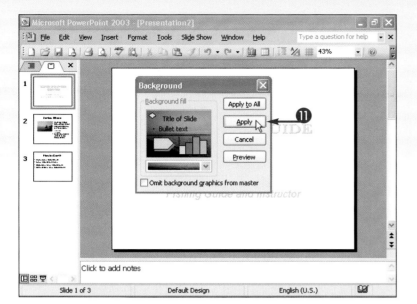

The Background
dialog box reappears.

⑪ Click Apply.

CONTINUED

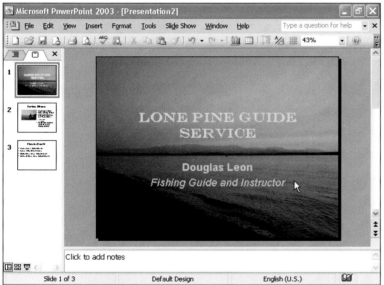

The background image is applied to the
slide.

TIPS

Apply It!

You can also apply a background image
to Notes Masters. To apply a
background image to a Notes Master,
click View, Master, and then Notes
Master. Next, follow steps **1** to **11**. Use
this option with caution because the
notes text will print on top of the
background image, which may affect
legibility.

Apply It!

If you want to apply your custom
background image to an entire
presentation, follow steps **1** to **10**, but
in step **11**, click Apply to All instead of
Apply. When you click Apply to All, the
background image is applied to all
pages, including the Slide Master.

Display Content in
DIFFERENT LANGUAGES

You can work with and edit content in any language supported by your Microsoft Windows operating system. The versions of Windows on which PowerPoint 2003 runs allow you to install support for most languages, including languages that are read from right to left and languages that require special keyboard mappings to produce characters that are not on standard U.S. English keyboards.

For example, if your Windows XP operating system is configured to support Japanese, then PowerPoint 2003 can display Japanese text using Japanese characters, and can check for spelling errors using Japanese proofing tools.

When some languages are enabled, new features are uncovered. The most common features are proofing tools like the spell checker. In addition, some languages enable new tools such as language-specific formatting options on the Format menu.

You can use the Microsoft Office 2003 Language Settings tool to enable language support in PowerPoint 2003. Once the tool enables support for specific languages and you identify specific text in one of those languages, you can take advantage of language-specific tools.

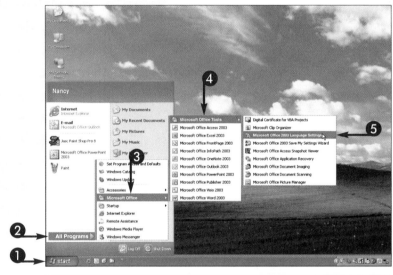

CONFIGURE OFFICE FOR MULTIPLE LANGUAGES

① Click Start.

② Click All Programs.

③ Click Microsoft Office.

④ Click Microsoft Office Tools.

⑤ Click Microsoft Office 2003 Language Settings.

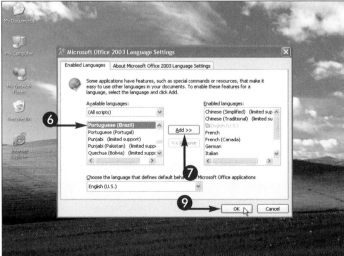

The Microsoft Office 2003 Language Settings dialog box appears.

⑥ In the Available languages section, scroll down and click the language you want to use.

⑦ Click Add to add languages to the Enabled languages section.

⑧ Repeat steps **6** and **7** for each language you want to enable.

⑨ Click OK.

The next time you use PowerPoint, you can work with content in different languages.

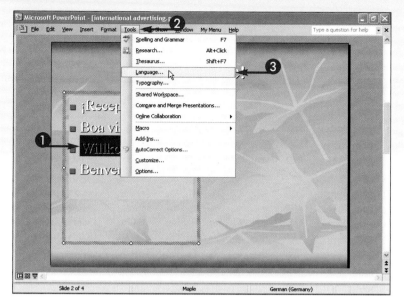

IDENTIFY TEXT AS A SPECIFIC LANGUAGE

① Click and drag to highlight the text that you want to mark as a particular language.

② Click Tools.

③ Click Language.

DIFFICULTY LEVEL

The Language dialog box appears.

④ In the Mark selected text as section, scroll down and click the language in which you want the selected text to appear.

⑤ Click OK.

The language of the selected text is changed.

Tools enabled by that language are now available for use.

TIPS

Did You Know?

You can mark all text for a specific language by clicking Edit, Select All, and then following steps **1** to **5** in the Identify Text as a Specific Language section above.

Caution!

Microsoft Windows system requirements differ for each language you want to use. For example, some languages that are read from right to left and some of the Asian languages have specific system requirements that must be met before you can type in those languages. However, you can open and display content in presentations that were created in any language in which Office has been enabled by using the Microsoft Office 2003 Language Settings tool.

Add Impact with Graphics

You can enhance the effectiveness of your presentations when you use graphics to help communicate your message. You can put content from your digital camera or scanner to work for you by inserting photos, drawings, and documents into your presentations. For example, if you have a printed photograph you would like to include on a slide, PowerPoint communicates directly with your scanner to scan the photograph and then insert it into your presentation.

Once your images or graphics are in your presentations, you can learn how to add effects to get them noticed. You can add colorful borders to make them stand out, and you can crop photos so that only the most important parts are included in your slides.

If you have ever wondered how to make an image with a white background blend in on a slide with a color background, you can use the Set Transparent Color tool to make it work. You can also add clarity to your presentation by adding text to AutoShapes or enhancing AutoShapes with three-dimensional effects. You can even learn how to compress graphics to manage the size of presentations and make them load more quickly.

You can create a Photo Album that displays a collection of images or photographs in one of many available styles. Photo Album presentations are professionally formatted and save you time because, after selecting which images to include, all of the work of preparing the presentation is done for you.

Top 100

Add interest with
DIGITAL CAMERA PICTURES

You can use images from your digital camera to enhance your presentations by giving them the look and feel you want. You can use images from digital cameras to illustrate specific points and to communicate an overall feeling or sentiment in introductory or summary slides.

Digital cameras are popular because the images they produce have improved to near-photo quality in even inexpensive models. The digital images they produce are easy to use in PowerPoint presentations. You can

use the software programs that come with most digital cameras to upload images from the camera to your computer's hard drive. The images are stored on your hard drive in a graphics file format, such as JPG or GIF, which are supported by most graphics editing programs. You can crop images, resize them, add text, and more. Because PowerPoint supports these file formats, you can easily insert the images into your presentations.

① Click Insert.

② Click Picture.

③ Click From File.

The Insert Picture dialog box appears.

④ Click here and select the folder where your image is located.

⑤ Click the image you want to insert.

⑥ Click Insert.

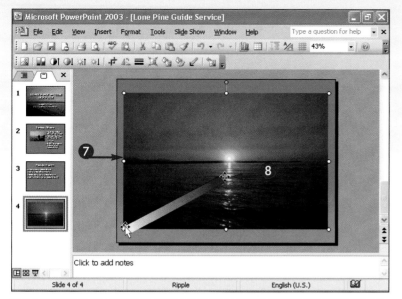

The image is inserted into the page at its original size.

⑦ Click the image to select it.

When you click the image, the image resizing handles become visible.

⑧ Click any corner of the image and drag it diagonally toward the opposite corner of the image to resize it.

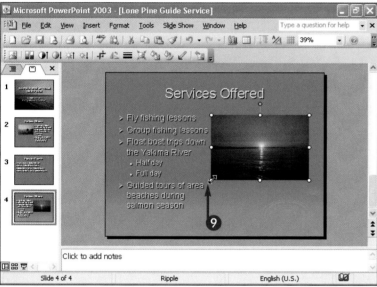

⑨ Click and drag the image to the desired location on the slide.

The image is positioned on the slide.

TIPS

Caution!

Digital cameras store images for printing at a quality higher than you need for presentations that will be viewed online. Higher-quality images result in larger file sizes; therefore, to keep your presentation loading quickly, you should compress your images whenever possible. See Task #21 for information on how to compress images.

Did You Know?

You can use formatting tools to draw attention to your images. The Picture toolbar includes tools for changing brightness, contrast, cropping, rotating, adding lines, and more. If the Picture toolbar is not visible, click View, Toolbars, and then Picture to make it visible.

Try This!

You can add a shadow effect to your images to make them stand out on your slides. To add a shadow effect on an image, first make sure that the Drawing toolbar is visible. If it is not, click View, Toolbars, and then Drawing. Click the image to which you want to apply a shadow, then click the Shadow Style button (▣), and then click the shadow style you want to apply.

SCAN DOCUMENTS
to convert into digital images

You can turn hard-copy photographs and other documents into digital images by using a scanner. Scanners convert documents, photographs, or other materials into electronic files. After the documents are scanned, they are usually stored as graphics files in formats such as TIF, JPG, and GIF.

PowerPoint combines the scanning of documents and inserting them into your presentations into an easy process. PowerPoint communicates with the scanner's software, which then communicates with the scanner to create the image. After creating the image, the

software passes the image to PowerPoint to be inserted into the presentation.

Scanned images are often high-quality graphics files that can be large in size. Large image files increase the size of your presentation and increase the time it takes to load. Scanned images, when inserted into slides, are usually displayed at their real size, which is often too large for your presentation. Insert the scanned image, resize it, and then compress it to decrease its size. To learn about compressing graphics, see Task #21.

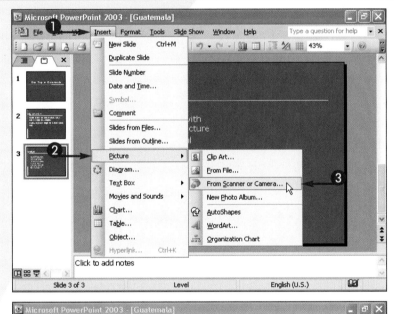

① Click Insert.

② Click Picture.

③ Click From Scanner or Camera.

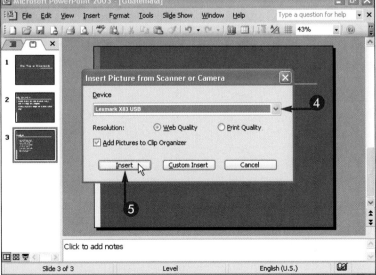

The Insert Picture from Scanner or Camera dialog box appears.

④ Click here and select the scanner you want to use to scan the image.

⑤ Click Insert.

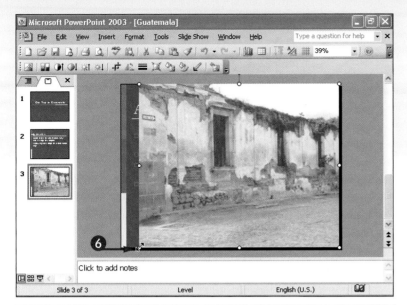

The scanner scans the image and then inserts it into the slide.

⑥ Click any corner of the image and drag it diagonally toward the opposite corner to resize it.

⑦ Click and drag the image to the desired location on the slide.

● The scanned image is positioned on the slide.

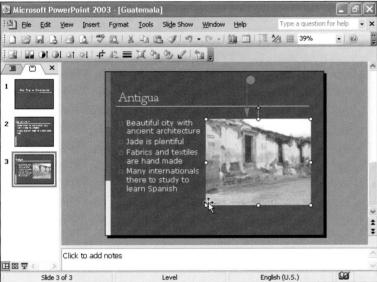

TIPS

Caution!

Images are scanned using the scanner's default settings. Change the scanner properties before scanning if the image area is too large or too small, or the color or clarity of the image is less than desired. Follow steps **1** to **4**, and then click Custom Insert. Your scanner's property settings dialog box appears. Follow the scanning procedures for your scanner, and then follow steps **6** and **7** above.

Print It!

You can scan your image at a high-quality resolution suitable for print. Simply follow steps **1** to **4** above, and then make sure that the Print Quality option is selected (○ changes to ◉) in the Resolution section.

Emphasize images with
BORDERS

You can make images in your presentations stand out when you add image borders. For example, in a presentation where the slide background color is similar to the colors used on an image on the slide, add a colorful image border to make the slide stand out against the background.

You can use image borders to highlight items that users can click for some other effect. Traditionally, items you can click on a Web site have a colorful highlighted border around them. If you add a

hyperlink to an image in PowerPoint, borders are not added automatically. You can go in and add borders to images that use effects like hyperlinks. For more information about adding hyperlinks to images, see Tasks #54 and #55.

Image borders in PowerPoint are simply lines placed around images. The true power in image borders is the ability to use virtually any color or any line width to make your image borders truly unique.

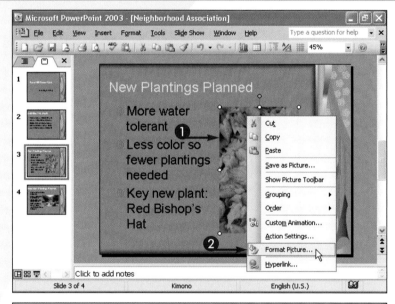

❶ Right-click the image.

The Edit menu appears.

❷ Click Format Picture.

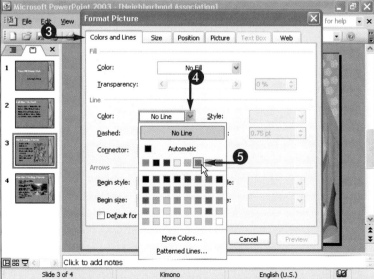

The Format Picture dialog box appears.

❸ Click the Colors and Lines tab.

❹ Click the Color ⩔.

❺ Click the color you want to use for the border in the Color area.

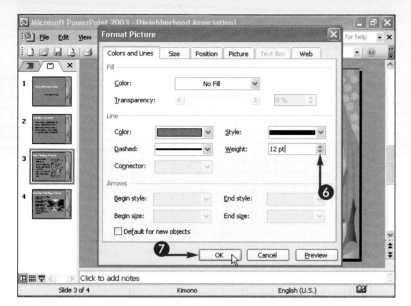

6 Click the Weight ![icon] to set the line weight.

7 Click OK.

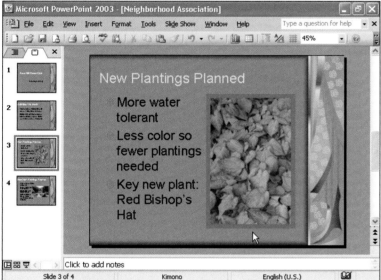

The image is updated with the new border.

TIPS

Did You Know?
Line weights are measured in points. A point is equivalent to ½ of an inch. A line that is 12 pixels high is 12 dots high, or the height of a capital letter I in a 12-point font.

Try It!
You can also use dashed or dotted lines for your borders. Follow steps **1** to **6** above, click the Dashed ![icon], and then click the dashed or dotted line you want to use.

Did You Know?
You can change the line style to one of the preset styles, such as ¼ point or double or triple lines. Follow steps **1** to **6** above, click the Style ![icon], and then click the style you want to use.

CROP IMAGES
to attract attention

You can attract attention to just the part of pictures or graphics that you want when you crop an image. You can think of cropping an image as similar to cutting the edges off a photograph or even cutting off unnecessary or unwanted parts of a photograph before you place it in a photo album. Cropping in PowerPoint is similar in that you remove the portions outside the area on which you want to focus.

Cropping is especially useful if you routinely add digital camera images to slides. Digital images are often sized at a ratio of 1:1.5. For example, an image that is 4" high will be 6" wide, or 4"x 6". If you want to display the image as a square, you can crop to reduce the width. You can crop almost any type of image, except for animated GIF files. For more information about inserting images from a digital camera into a presentation, see Task #17.

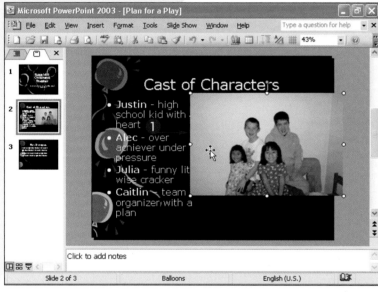

① Click the image you want to crop.

② Click View.

③ Click Toolbars.

④ Click Picture.

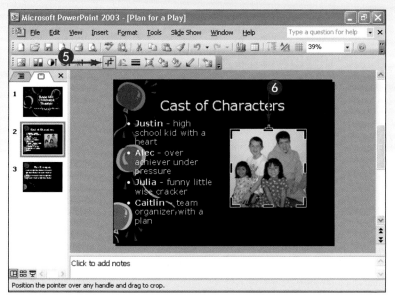

The Picture toolbar appears.

5 Click the Crop button on the Picture toolbar.

The cropping handles appear on the picture.

6 Click one of the cropping handles, and then drag toward the center of the picture.

Repeat step **6** for each side or corner you want to crop.

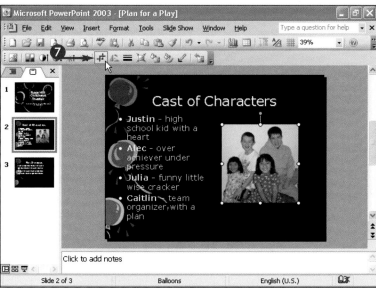

7 Click the Crop button on the Picture toolbar.

The image is cropped.

TIPS

Did You Know?

After you crop an image it will appear smaller, but it will not take up less space in your presentation until you compress it. To learn more about compressing images, see Task #21.

Apply It!

After you crop an image, you can reposition it on the screen if you want. Follow steps **1** to **6** above, and then click and drag the image to the location you want.

Move It!

When you open the Picture toolbar, you may find that it is floating on the screen. If you want to dock it on a menu bar, click the dark blue area at the top of the toolbar and then drag it onto a menu bar area.

COMPRESS GRAPHICS
to make presentations load faster

You can compress graphics from within PowerPoint to minimize the size of graphics files. Compressing graphics files is a good idea because the smaller presentation file sizes are, the faster presentations download and open.

Graphics should be compressed after they are manipulated in PowerPoint. For example, if you scan an image into a presentation, it is likely to be a high-quality file suitable for print, but may include more richness than can be displayed on standard monitors or projectors. If your presentation is likely to be

viewed on monitors rather than printed, you can compress the images for Web or screen resolution.

Even if you expect to print your presentations with high quality, you should compress graphics if they have been resized or cropped. When you resize or crop images, the visual image of the graphics file changes, but the actual size of the file remains unchanged. The Compress Pictures tool removes cropped or resized portions of images from files and decreases the file size.

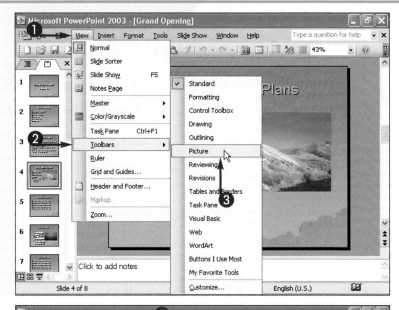

① Click View.

② Click Toolbars.

③ Click Picture.

The Picture toolbar appears.

④ Click the image to compress.

⑤ Click the Compress Pictures button on the Picture toolbar.

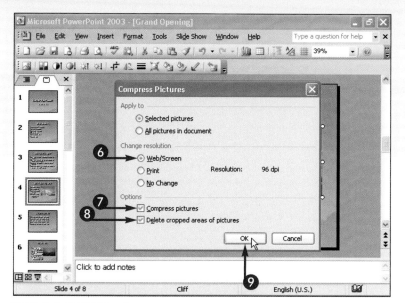

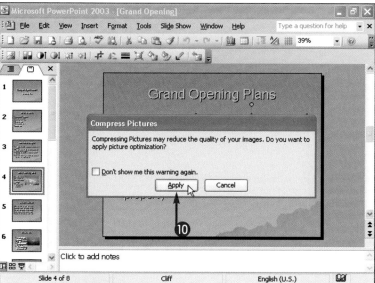

The Compress Pictures dialog box appears.

⑥ In the Change resolution section, click the Web/Screen option (○ changes to ⊙).

⑦ In the Options section, click the Compress pictures option (☐ changes to ☑).

⑧ In the Options section, click the Delete cropped areas of pictures option (☐ changes to ☑).

⑨ Click OK.

The Compress Pictures warning appears.

⑩ Click Apply.

The image is compressed

Did You Know?

You can choose to maintain the screen resolution of existing images that you compress after they have been resized or cropped. Follow steps **1** to **10** above, but in step **6** make sure that the No Change option is selected (○ changes to ⊙).

Caution!

You can easily compress all pictures in your presentation at once. Simply follow the steps above, but before step **6**, in the Apply to section, make sure that the All pictures in document option is selected (○ changes to ⊙) instead of the Selected pictures option. Use caution, though. These settings will be applied to all pictures in your presentation.

Display pictures in a
PHOTO ALBUM

You can quickly create a photo album presentation to display images or graphics in a variety of styles. The Photo Album tool creates a brand-new presentation with the photos and graphics you select arranged on each slide. The images you choose can be in any file format that is supported by PowerPoint, and it is not necessary for the files to be located in the same directory.

The Photo Album tool saves time because it allows you to insert many images at once and then formats

the slides with the selected number of pictures. For example, without the Photo Album tool, if you wanted to arrange six images on two slides, you would have to create the slides, insert the images into the presentation, and then you would have to resize and reposition the images on the two slides. The Photo Album tool performs these tasks for you and applies selected special effects to the images, such as corner tabs or special shapes.

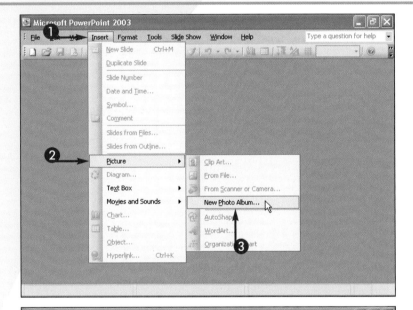

① Click Insert.

② Click Picture.

③ Click New Photo Album.

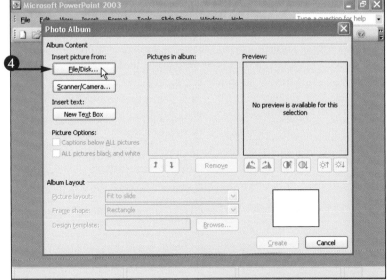

The Photo Album dialog box appears.

④ Click File/Disk.

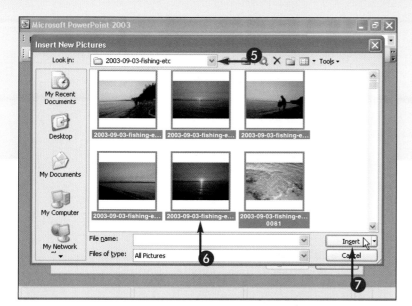

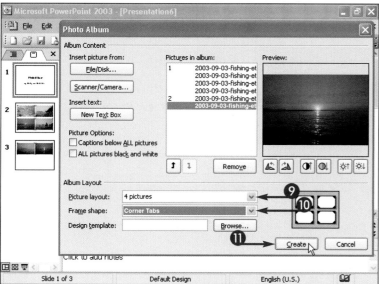

The Insert New Pictures dialog box appears.

⑤ Click here, and select the file folder where your image is located.

⑥ Click the file you want to insert into your photo album.

Note: You can Ctrl+Click to select more than one file at a time.

⑦ Click Insert.

⑧ Repeat steps **4** to **7** if you want to insert more images.

The Insert New Pictures dialog box disappears.

⑨ Click here and select the Picture layout you want to use.

⑩ Click here and select the Frame shape that you want to use.

⑪ Click Create.

A new presentation is created with the photos displayed in a photo album style.

TIPS

Did You Know?
After you have created a photo album presentation, you can make changes to it. Simply click Format, and then Photo Album.

Did You Know?
You can copy slides created with the Photo Album tool into an existing presentation. However, you lose the ability to edit the pages that have been copied.

Customize It!
You can create your photo album using a Design Layout for a more professional look. Follow steps **1** to **11** above, and then click the Browse button next to Design Template. Double-click the Presentation Designs folder to open it. Click the Design Layout you want to use, and then click Select.

BLEND GRAPHICS
into the background

You can make parts of a graphic transparent against a colored background by using the Set Transparent Color option. The Set Transparent Color option is helpful if you are placing an image or logo onto a slide that is not rectangular and has a background color different from the background color used in your slide. Images that do not have irregular edges, such as rectangles, are not usually good candidates for using the Transparency option because rectangular images are easily cropped, while images with irregular or angular edges are difficult to crop. See Task #20 for more information about cropping.

The Set Transparent Color option works when you click in an area of the image that contains the single color that you want to become transparent. After you click the color that you want to make transparent, every instance of that color in the image is made transparent, allowing the background color or image to show through. The Set Transparent Color option can be used with most images supported by PowerPoint except for animated GIF files.

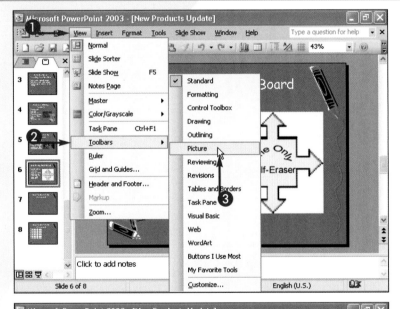

① Click View.

② Click Toolbars.

③ Click Picture.

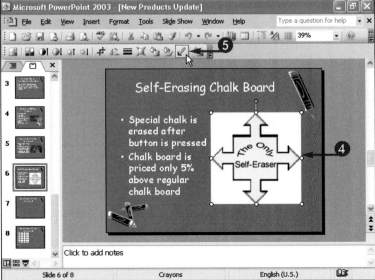

The Picture toolbar appears.

④ Click the image.

⑤ Click the Set Transparent Color tool on the Picture toolbar.

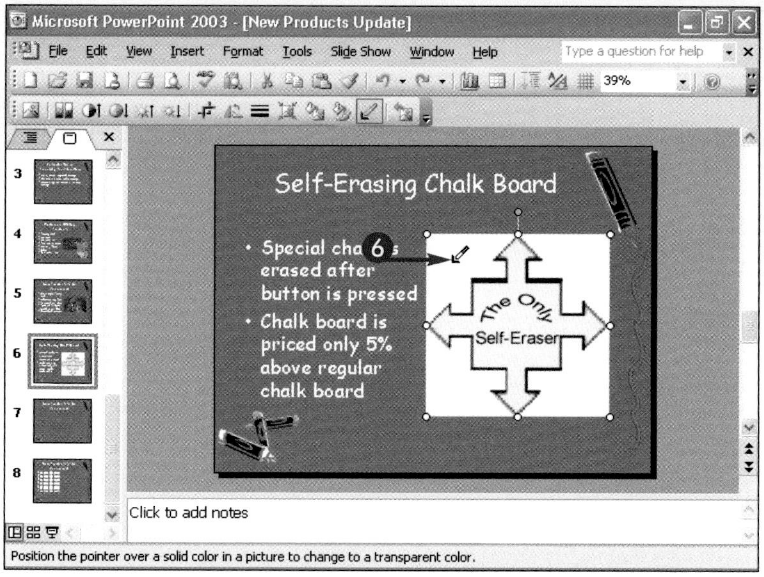

The changes to .

6 Click the color in the image that you want to become transparent.

#23

DIFFICULTY LEVEL

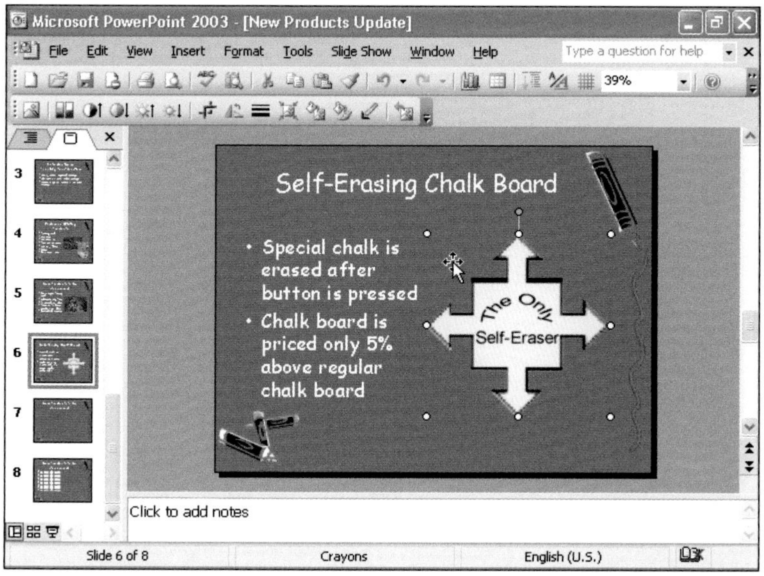

The color you clicked is transparent.

TIPS

Attention!

Many images, especially photographs, appear to have a uniform background color, when in reality there are slight variations in color. When the Set Transparent Color option is used on these images, not all of the background is made transparent.

Caution!

The Set Transparent Color option makes all instances of the selected color transparent. If that color is included in the main part of the graphic, it will also be made transparent.

Did You Know?

If you do not get the desired results with the Set Transparent Color option, you can use a graphic editing program to create transparent GIF images. These images already have areas defined to be transparent so you will not need to use the Set Transparent Color option.

Add text to your
AUTOSHAPES

You can insert text into most AutoShapes in order to convey important messages more clearly. AutoShapes make it easy to add arrows, stars, banners, callout boxes, and more to slides. Without text in the AutoShapes, however, a user viewing your presentation online or in printed format might not understand the point of an AutoShape. For example, an AutoShape arrow may focus attention on an important part of a chart or graph, but without text on the arrow, the user might have a difficult time understanding why it is important.

Did You Know?

AutoShapes carry the most impact when the design of the AutoShape conveys an important message. If the text itself is much more important than the design of the AutoShape, consider adding WordArt, which adds highly formatted text to slides, rather than an AutoShape.

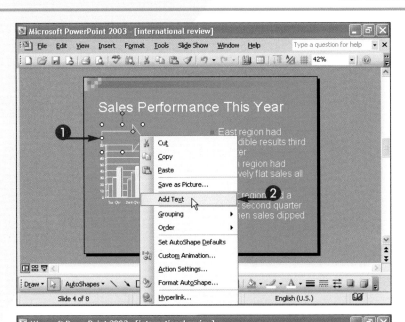

① Right-click on the AutoShape to which you want to add text.

The Edit menu appears.

② Click Add Text.

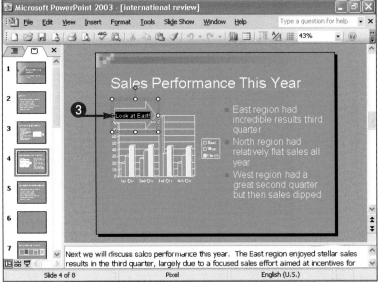

An insertion point is added to the graphic.

③ Type the desired text.

USE 3-D EFFECTS
to make graphics stand out

You can add 3-D effects to AutoShapes to make them appear three-dimensional by using the 3-D Style button (□) on the Drawing toolbar. Three-dimensional effects make graphics more attention getting because they add depth and an additional layer of color to slides.

3-D effects add shadows to AutoShapes to help make them look truly three-dimensional. 3-D effects automatically use the coloring scheme that is used on the slide on which the AutoShape appears so that the effects are coordinated with other slide content.

TIP

Caution!
Although you can apply 3-D effects to most AutoShapes, you cannot apply 3-D Styles to some graphics files like photos imported from a digital camera. You can use the Shadow tool (□), which is also available on the Drawing toolbar, to add dimension to images and other graphics files.

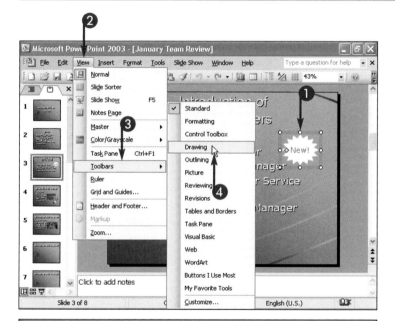

① Click the AutoShape to which you want to add a 3-D effect.

② Click View.

③ Click Toolbars.

④ Click Drawing.

The Drawing toolbar appears.

⑤ Click the 3-D Style button on the Drawing toolbar.

⑥ Click the desired 3-D effect.

The 3-D effect is applied to the image.

Use Timesaving Tools

You can accomplish work faster in PowerPoint with tools that can help make routine work less tedious. For example, if you have ever become tired of retyping the same names or phrases repeatedly, you can use AutoCorrect to replace abbreviations with complete phrases, titles, or names. You can also reduce errors by instructing PowerPoint to fix the most common typographical errors automatically as you type.

You can eliminate guesswork by using the Format Painter to copy text and graphics effects from one place to another in your presentation. You can even turn one of your favorite presentations into a Design Template that you can use to create future presentations.

If you go to a Web site to do research and then become distracted by all of the options available online, PowerPoint's Research Task Pane helps you stay focused and on task. Its Internet search capabilities reduce distractions and bring you the tools you need where you need them. You can even use the Research Pane to look up words or phrases in the online dictionary or thesaurus, or translate words from language to language.

If you have ever wondered if there is a faster way to perform repetitive tasks, macros can help. The Macro Recorder in PowerPoint allows you to easily convert mouse clicks and keystrokes into Visual Basic for Applications code to help automate tasks.

PASTE SLIDES
from one presentation to another

You can easily copy and then paste slides from one presentation to another. When you copy slides they are placed onto the Office Clipboard where they are stored until you either collect 24 more items or clear items from the Office Clipboard. This allows you to copy slides, text, and graphics from a variety of presentations first, and then selectively paste them when you are ready. If you choose not to use the Office Clipboard, you can paste the slides as long as they were the last item copied or cut. To learn more about the Office Clipboard, see Task #6.

The Slide Sorter View and the slide tab on the Normal View are the most convenient places to copy slides because the thumbnail images allow you to select and then copy more than one slide at a time. When you copy slides from one presentation to another, by default, the copied slides take on the formatting of the new presentation. You can also choose to maintain the existing format of the copied slides.

① Click to select the slides you want to copy.

Note: *You can press Ctrl+click to select more than one slide.*

② Click the Copy button.

You can also press Ctrl+C to copy the slides to the Clipboard.

③ Click Window.

④ Click the presentation to which you want to copy the slides.

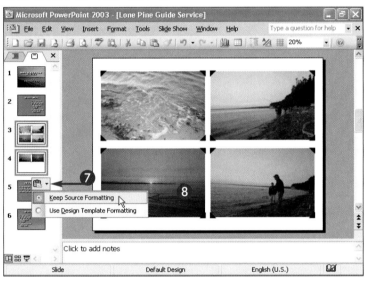

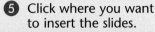

The presentation where you want to insert the slides appears.

⑤ Click where you want to insert the slides.

⑥ Click the Paste button.

You can also press Ctrl+V to paste the slides.

The slides are pasted into the presentation. The Paste Options Smart Tag appears.

DIFFICULTY LEVEL

⑦ Click the Paste Options ▾.

The Paste Options are displayed.

⑧ Click the Keep Source Formatting option (○ changes to ◉).

The slides return to their source format.

TIPS

Did You Know?

You can paste slides from the Office Clipboard by clicking View, Task Pane, and then the Task Pane ▾. Click Clipboard, and the Office Clipboard opens. Click where you would like to insert the slides in Slide Sorter or Slide tab in Normal View; then click the ▾ on the Office Clipboard next to the slides you would like to paste. Click Paste.

Apply It!

You can selectively copy more than one slide at a time by viewing slides in the Slide tab in Normal View, and then Ctrl+clicking for each slide you want to select. When you finish selecting slides, press Ctrl+C to copy them.

USE AUTOCORRECT
to save typing time

You can reduce errors by letting PowerPoint automatically correct common typing mistakes for you. AutoCorrect maintains a list of mistyped words, as well as a list of the correct words used to replace them. When a word on the Replace list is typed and then a space or end punctuation mark is typed, the word is automatically replaced with the correct word from the Replace With list.

You can also use AutoCorrect to save time by adding abbreviations for commonly used titles, names, and phrases to the Replace list, and then specifying the

longer text with which to replace them. For example, a neighborhood association worker can create an AutoCorrect entry to automatically replace *RHNA* with *Rose Hill Neighborhood Association* to save time and make typing such a long title easier and less prone to errors.

You can also use AutoCorrect to correctly capitalize words or phrases. For example, you can add correctly spelled words to the AutoCorrect list that are capitalized correctly when typed.

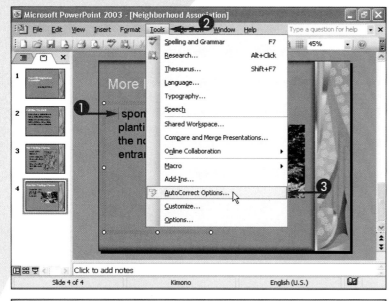

① Click where you want to insert the AutoCorrect text.

② Click Tools.

③ Click AutoCorrect Options.

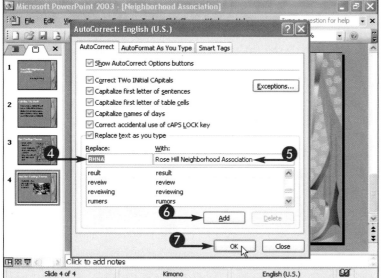

The AutoCorrect dialog box appears.

④ Type your AutoCorrect shortcut in the Replace field.

⑤ Type the text you want to replace the AutoCorrect shortcut when typed in the With field.

⑥ Click Add.

⑦ Click OK.

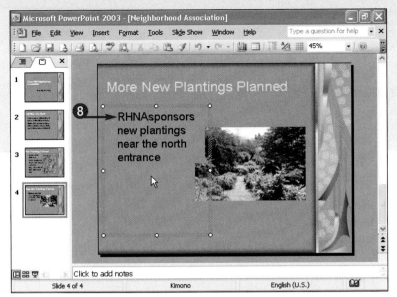

The AutoCorrect dialog box closes.

⑧ Type the AutoCorrect shortcut, and then press the spacebar.

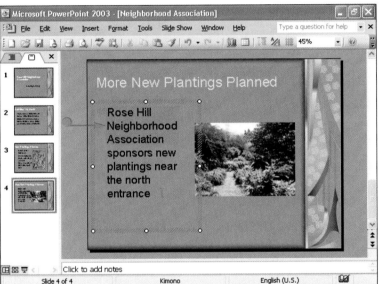

● The AutoCorrect shortcut is replaced with the AutoCorrect text.

TIPS

Did You Know?
You can specify exceptions to the list of words to automatically correct. For example, you can specify not to automatically capitalize words that follow an abbreviation. This would prevent a phrase as *It is 6 ft. high* from being changed to *It is 6 ft. High* because of the period following the abbreviation. To add exceptions, follow steps **1** to **3** above, and then click Exceptions on the AutoCorrect dialog box. After you have specified exceptions, continue with steps **4** to **8** above.

Did You Know?
You can use AutoCorrect when you enable other languages in PowerPoint. To learn more about enabling PowerPoint for other languages, see Task #16.

COPY EFFECTS
from one image to another

You can easily transfer formatting from one area of text to another with the Format Painter. The Format Painter is a tool on the Formatting toolbar that allows you to click one piece of text, copy the formatting of that text, and then apply that formatting to another piece of text. The Format Painter does not copy the text, just the formatting of the text.

The Format Painter is especially useful when you open a presentation that you did not create, and you do not know what fonts, font styles, and other

formatting were used when it was created. For example, if some text in your presentation uses a custom color and a font that is unfamiliar to you, you save time by simply using the Format Painter to copy the formatting and apply it to your presentation. Without the Format Painter, you would have to look up the RGB value of the color used, then look up the formatting used, and then manually apply the color and the special formatting to the text.

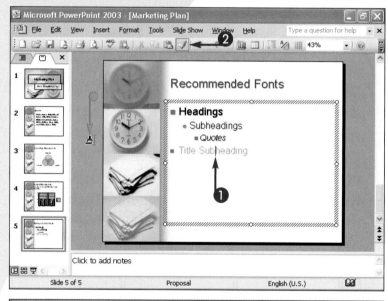

① Click the text from which you want to copy the format.

② Click the Format Painter button on the Standard toolbar.

● The ⌖ changes to the 🖌.

③ Click the slide that contains the text to which you want to apply the copied format.

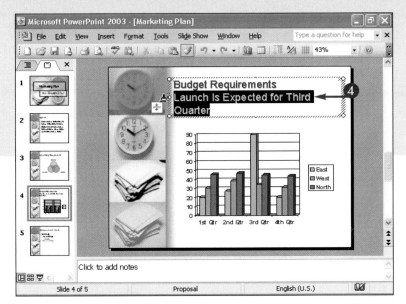

The slide opens.

④ Click and drag to highlight the text to which you want to apply the copied format.

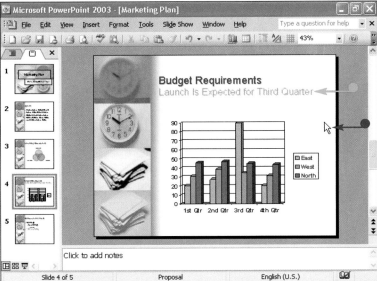

● The format is copied from one area of text to another.

● The 📋 changes back to ⌖.

Did You Know?

You can also use the Format Painter when you have an AutoShape in your presentation that has been formatted with colors, shadows, gradients, and other effects that could be difficult to identify and then reproduce on another AutoShape or image. You can follow the steps above to copy formatting from one image or AutoShape to another.

Did You Know?

You can also use the Format Painter to copy and then paste formats from one presentation to another. Make sure that both presentations are open. Follow steps **1** and **2** above, and then switch to the slide in the other presentation that contains the text you want to change, and follow steps **3** and **4** above.

SEARCH THE INTERNET
from within PowerPoint

You can research Internet Web sites from within PowerPoint to save time and stay focused on your work. The Research Task Pane appears to the right of the PowerPoint work area so that you can continue to work on your presentations while you research.

You can also click and drag the Research Task Pane to other positions on the screen, including floating on top of the work area. When you use the Research Task Pane, search results are displayed within the Task Pane. The Research Task Pane is preconfigured

to search popular online reference books, research sites, business and financial sites, and sites you add to the list.

Much like an Internet browser, you can click the Back and Forward buttons in the Research Task Pane to help you navigate through research results. You can click hyperlinks to Web pages that are in the search results to open Internet Explorer with the same Task Pane positioned so that you can continue your research when desired.

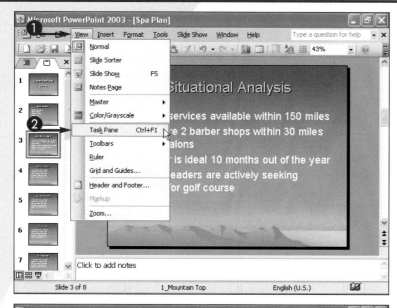

① Click View.

② Click Task Pane.

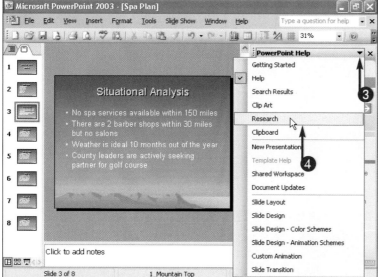

The Task Pane appears.

③ Click the Task Pane ▼.

④ Click Research.

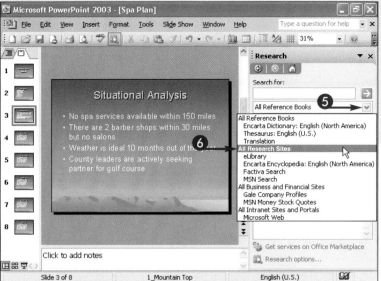

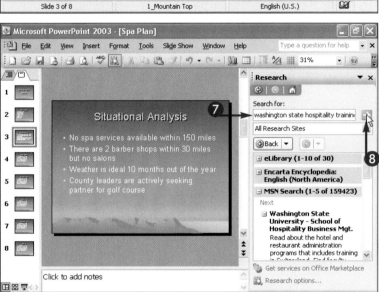

⑦ Type the term you want to search for in the Search for field.

⑧ Click →.

Search results are displayed in the Research Task Pane.

TIPS

Did You Know?
You can add or remove Web sites from the list of reference options in the Research Task Pane. Click the Research options link on the Research Task Pane, and then make sure that there is a checkmark (☑) next to each option you want to use on the Research Options dialog box. To add a site, click the Add Services button on the Research Options dialog box. Type the Web site address of the site you want to add in the Address field, click Add, and then click OK.

Did You Know?
You can quickly open the Research Task Pane by pressing Alt and then clicking a word that you want to look up.

LOOK UP WORDS
in the dictionary

You can find the meaning and pronunciation of words by looking them up in the online dictionary that is accessible from the Research Task Pane in PowerPoint. The Research Task Pane opens to the right of the work area in PowerPoint, allowing you to look up words while continuing to work on your presentation.

You can look for words by selecting Encarta Dictionary in the list of research options. When you submit a word, the word's definitions and pronunciations are listed in the Task Pane with a list

of alternative research options. The research portion of the Research Task Pane works much like an Internet browser with forward and back buttons that allow you to easily move through your research.

You can also choose to find words in the online Thesaurus, which provides you a list of words that are similar in meaning to the ones you are researching. You can access the Thesaurus in the All Reference Books portion of the research options list in the Research Task Pane.

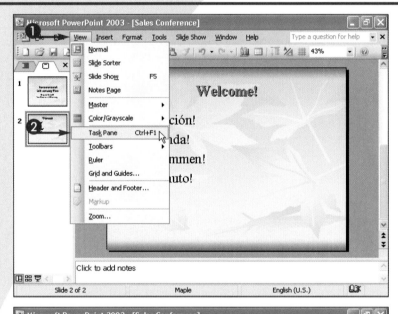

① Click View.

② Click Task Pane.

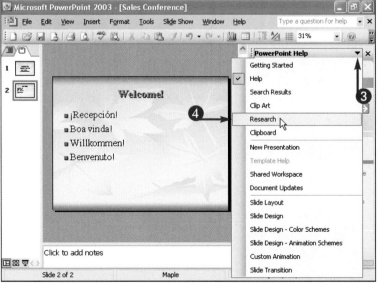

The Task Pane appears.

③ Click the Task Pane ▼.

④ Click Research.

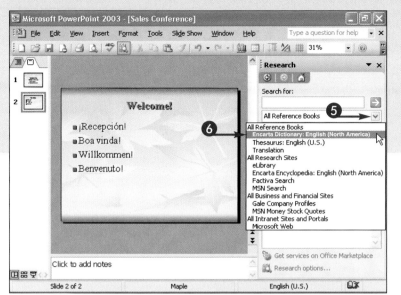

The Research Task Pane appears.

⑤ Click the Research Options ☑.

⑥ Click the Encarta Dictionary option.

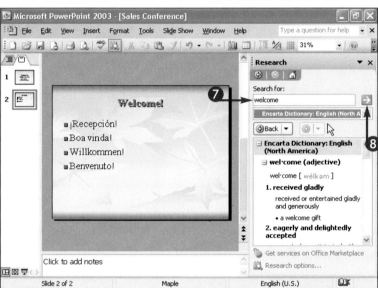

⑦ Type the word you want to look up in the Search for field.

⑧ Click ➡.

Search results appear in the Research Task Pane.

TIPS

Did You Know?

More online dictionaries are available on the Internet. To add one to the list of available reference services, click the Research options button on the Research Task Pane. Click the Add Services button on the Research Options dialog box, type the address of the Web site you want to add in the Address field, click Add, and then click OK.

Find It

You can also look up a word in the Encarta Dictionary by right-clicking it and then clicking Look Up. The Research Task Pane opens with search results displayed.

Did You Know?

You can easily look up words in the online Thesaurus by right-clicking the word and then clicking Synonyms from the menu that appears.

TRANSLATE WORDS
from within PowerPoint

You can translate words from one language to another by using the Research Task Pane in PowerPoint. The Research Task Pane enables you to see translation results in various forms, such as nouns, verbs, or adjectives. The next time you select the Translation option on the Research Task Pane, the languages chosen on the last search are presented again so that it is not necessary to repeat language selections unless you want to change the languages to use for the translation.

Translation results appear in the Research Task Pane to the right of the PowerPoint work area. This allows you to continue working while you translate words. You can reposition the Research Task Pane by clicking and dragging it to another area on the screen.

The Research Task Pane also displays additional fee-based options for translation services. You can use the built-in translation tool for translating a few words. For longer documents, however, machine or human translation services can be more accurate.

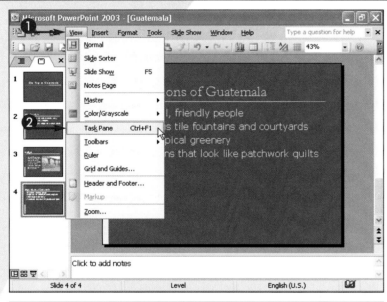

1 Click View.

2 Click Task Pane.

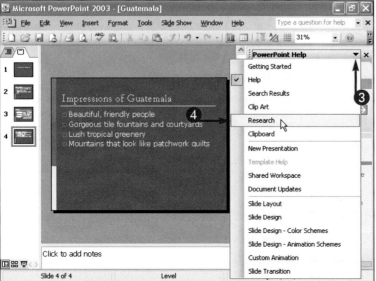

The Task Pane appears.

3 Click the Task Pane ▼.

4 Click Research.

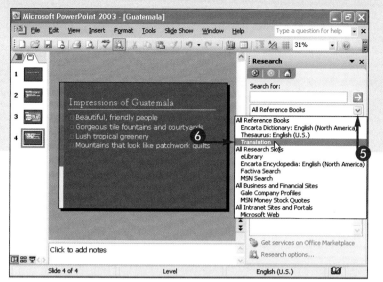

The Research Task Pane appears.

5 Click the Research Options ☑.

6 Click the Translation option.

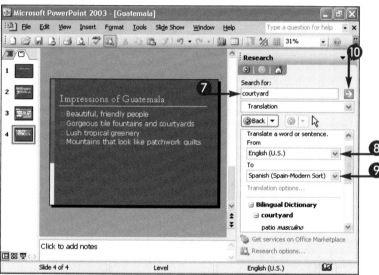

7 Type the word you want to translate in the Search for field.

8 Click the From ☑ and select the language from which you want to translate the word.

9 Click the To ☑ and select the language to which you want to translate the word.

10 Click ➡.

Search results are displayed in the Research Task Pane.

Caution!
You may be prompted to install translation services if you have not done so already. If prompted, click Yes to install the services. For example, the first time you use the Research Task Pane to translate a word from Spanish to German, you may be prompted to install the service. Afterward, the Bilingual Dictionary is accessible.

Did You Know?
You can access translation services by right-clicking the word or phrase you want to translate, and then clicking Look Up. The Research Task Pane opens with the word looked up in the Encarta Dictionary. If you click the plus sign (+) next to the Translation section, you can choose to translate the word or phrase into another language.

Turn your presentation into a
DESIGN TEMPLATE

You can convert a favorite presentation into a Design Template that you can use to create new presentations. After you create a custom Design Template, it is made available along with the default Design Templates in the Slide Design Task Pane.

Custom Design Templates are especially useful if you have spent time customizing a presentation with the background colors, images, fonts, formatting, and graphics you like. Instead of copying and pasting an existing presentation, and then taking the time to replace all of the content, you can create a new

Design Template and use as the foundation for a new presentation.

You can also create custom Design Templates that are variations of an existing Design Template. For example, you may find that you like the Pixels Design Template, but want to change the color scheme and fonts to match your company's preferences. Instead of using the default Pixels Design Template and changing it each time, you can make your modifications once and make them forever available in the Slide Design Task Pane.

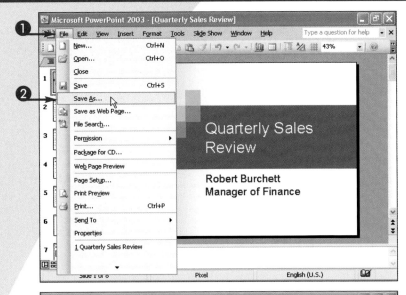

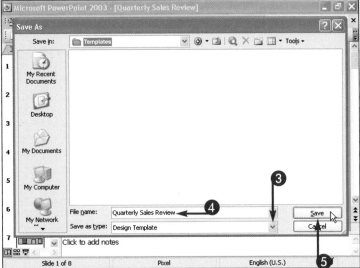

SAVE A PRESENTATION AS A CUSTOM DESIGN TEMPLATE

1 Click File.

2 Click Save As.

The Save As dialog box appears.

3 Click here and select Design Template.

4 Type the name of your custom Design Template in the File name field.

5 Click Save.

Your presentation is saved as a custom Design Template.

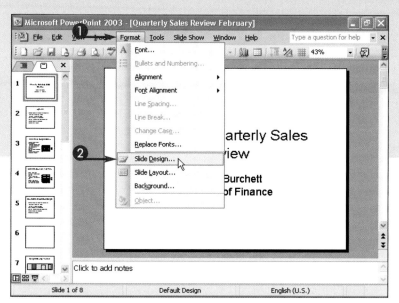

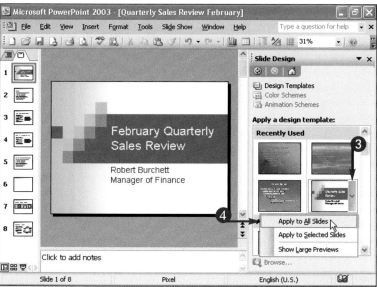

1 Click Format.

2 Click Slide Design.

The Slide Design Task Pane appears.

3 Click ⫶ next to your custom Design Template.

4 Click Apply to All Slides.

The custom Design Template is applied to all slides in your presentation.

TIPS

Apply It!

You can choose to apply your custom Design Template to selected slides instead of all slides. Follow steps **1** to **3** to apply a custom Design Template to a presentation, but in step **4**, click Apply to Selected Slides instead of Apply to All Slides.

Did You Know?

Design Templates are stored on your hard drive. For example, your Windows XP templates are in the c:\documents and settings\<**your profile**>\application data\Microsoft\templates directory. If you want to delete a Design Template, you should delete it by browsing to this location in Windows Explorer and then deleting it. If you are unable to see the application data directory, you may need to change your folder options to Show Hidden Files and Folders. For further instructions, see Windows help.

RECORD A MACRO
to automate repetitive tasks

You can save time when you frequently repeat common operations by creating a macro. A macro contains one or more instructions that perform tasks you would normally do with your mouse or keyboard, such as clicking menu or toolbar options.

Macros are usually created to help speed up tasks with many steps or tasks that require clicking options on several menus. For example, if you have a long presentation to edit and want to change line spacing on each slide, insert a logo, add a comment, and

then insert the date the presentation is changed, you can record a macro to perform these operations for you.

The Office Macro Recorder turns on when you create a macro and records your mouse clicks and keyboard operations. The Macro Recorder turns off when you click the Stop Macro button on the Stop Macro toolbar. The Macro Recorder converts the mouse clicks and keyboard operations into Visual Basic for Applications (VBA) commands. When the macro runs, it performs the same tasks that were recorded.

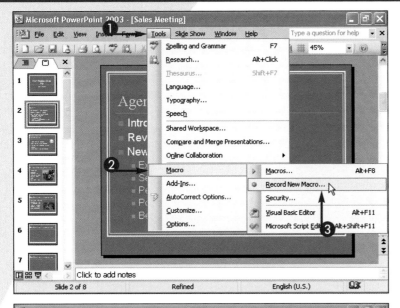

① Click Tools.

② Click Macro.

③ Click Record New Macro.

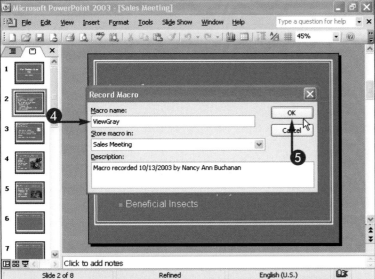

The Record Macro dialog box appears.

④ Type the name of your macro in the Macro name field.

⑤ Click OK.

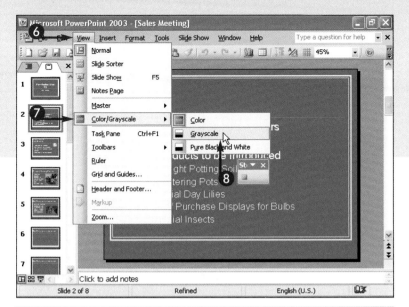

The Stop Macro toolbar appears.

Note: Steps **6** to **8** are the steps for recording a macro to change the view to gray. You may substitute the steps for the macro you want to record in steps **6** to **8**.

DIFFICULTY LEVEL

⑥ Click View.

⑦ Click Color/Grayscale.

⑧ Click Grayscale.

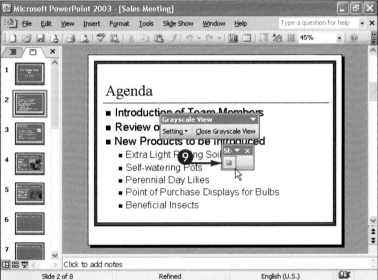

The screen changes to grayscale and the Grayscale View toolbar appears.

⑨ Click the Stop button on the Stop Macro toolbar.

The macro is recorded.

TIPS

Caution!
The Macro Recorder records mouse clicks and keyboard operations, but does not record mouse movements. Therefore, you must perform some operations with the keyboard instead of the mouse in order to record properly. For example, you can highlight text by pressing F8 instead of using the mouse.

Caution!
The Macro Recorder records all of the steps you take, including mistakes. You can either rerecord your macro or learn how to edit macros in Task #35.

Did You Know?
You can choose to store a macro in any open presentation. Perform steps **1** to **9** above. Following step **4**, click the Store macro in ⊡ and select the name of your open presentation before continuing.

Caution!
Macro names cannot include spaces or illegal characters such as !, @, #, $, %, or ^.

RUN A MACRO

to automate your functions

You can easily run a macro that helps automate common functions. Macros are commands that instruct PowerPoint to perform tasks that you would normally accomplish with mouse clicks and keyboard operations.

Macros are most commonly used to automate tasks that would otherwise require multiple steps or require accessing multiple menus or toolbars. For example, you could use a macro to insert a picture, resize the picture, and add a border around it every time it is run. Writing macros takes some expertise, but running a macro requires only a few steps.

Macros can greatly help save time and make working with programs like PowerPoint more efficient, but they have also proven to be a great way to spread computer viruses. You should enable and use macros only in presentations created by you or another trusted person, or programs that come from a company that has digitally signed it. Digital signatures come from certification authorities and allow you to find the vendor that produced a macro or program if there are virus or other security issues with it.

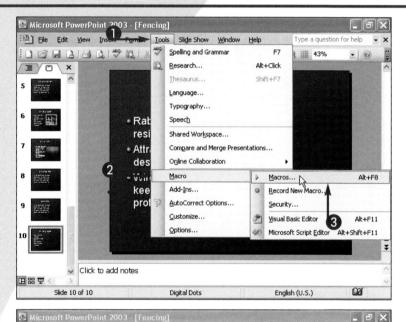

① Click Tools.

② Click Macro.

③ Click Macros.

The Macro dialog box appears.

④ Click the Macro in ▾.

⑤ Click All open presentations.

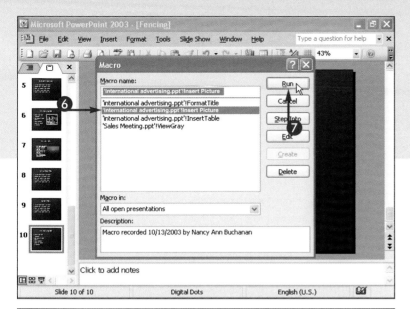

⑥ Click the macro name in the Macro name field.

⑦ Click Run.

The macro runs, and, in this example, the picture is inserted, resized, and a border is placed around it.

TIPS

Try This!
If you want to run a macro that is stored in the presentation you currently have open, follow steps **1** to **3** above; then click the macro name from the Macro Name field in the Macro dialog box. Proceed with step **7** to run the macro.

Did You Know?
You can see the security options available to you when you click Tools, Macros, and then Security. By default, security is set on High, which disables unsigned macros. You can list publishers from whom you trust macros on the Trusted Publishers tab.

Apply It!
You can place frequently used macros on toolbars to make them even easier to run. Click Tools and then Customize. In the Customize dialog box, click the Commands tab, and then click Macros in the Categories section. Click and drag the macros listed in the Commands section to the toolbar on which you want them to appear.

EDIT A MACRO
in the Visual Basic Editor

You can use the Microsoft Visual Basic Editor to edit an existing macro. When macros are recorded using the Macro Recorder, actions performed are converted into Visual Basic for Applications. The Visual Basic Editor is the tool for editing Visual Basic for Applications, and it comes with PowerPoint.

Because the Macro Recorder records all keystrokes and mouse movements, including mistakes, you may want to use the Visual Basic Editor to make edits. You do not need to know how to develop applications in Visual Basic to be able to tell what line

accomplishes what tasks in the macro, so editing the macro involves identifying the tasks and then deleting or modifying them as you see fit.

If your macro is complex and you are finding it difficult to accurately edit the macro with the Visual Basic Editor, you might want to consider simply rerecording the macro using the Macro Recorder. The Macro Recorder continues to record until you are finished, so there is no hurry to complete macros. You can find out more about the Macro Recorder in Task #33.

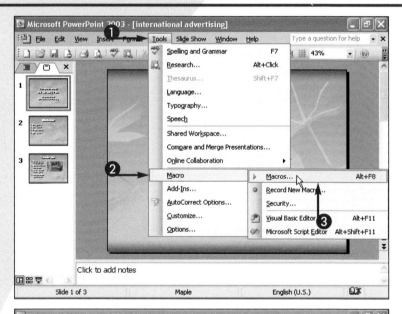

① Click Tools.

② Click Macro.

③ Click Macros.

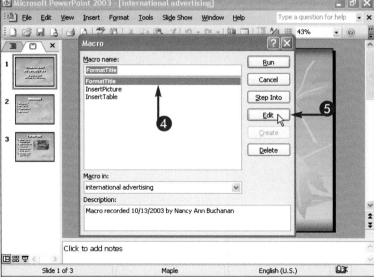

The Macro dialog box appears.

④ Click the name of the macro in the Macro name field.

⑤ Click Edit.

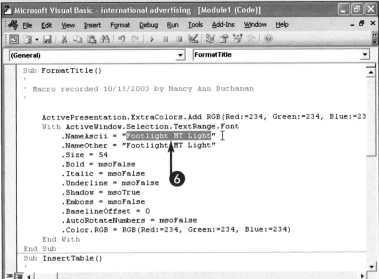

The macro opens in the Microsoft Visual Basic Editor.

⑥ Click and type to make your edits.

● The edits are reflected in the code.

⑦ Click the Save button.

⑧ Click the View Microsoft PowerPoint button.

Microsoft Visual Basic Editor closes.

TIPS

Get Help!

The Microsoft Visual Basic Editor includes a detailed help file to help you learn more about how to edit macros. You can access it from the Visual Basic Editor by clicking Help and then clicking Microsoft Visual Basic Help.

Apply It!

If you are having trouble identifying where a problem exists in your macro, try using Step Into. Step Into highlights each task in the macro and could help you identify separate tasks. Click Debug and then Step Into in the Visual Basic Editor.

Did You Know?

When you edit a macro, the Visual Basic Editor lists all of the macros that are stored in a presentation. You can edit all the macros in the same file.

Add Sizzle to Your Presentation with Effects

You can use effects on your slides to create presentations that sizzle. You can apply a shadow effect to transform an image that blends into the background into something that appears to pop off the slide.

You can anticipate questions and prepare to answer them when you insert hyperlinks in text or images that link to other places in your presentation. You can even create a button that opens another program and another document when clicked.

You can create visually stunning presentations that use animation effects to add movement and interest. You can also add entrance or exit effects to text or graphics to help explain

complex concepts or illustrate relationships. For example, you can demonstrate sequences of events when you bring an AutoShape into a slide, explain it, and then click to remove the AutoShape and simultaneously replace it with another. In fact, you can choreograph multiple effects to occur on each slide just when and where you want them.

You can make your presentations look more professional by using transition effects to gracefully remove one slide and replace it with another. To enhance your presentation even more, you can apply one of the pre-built Animation Schemes to automatically apply transition, exit, entrance, and motion path effects to every slide in your presentation.

Top 100

Highlight graphics when you use
CUSTOM SHADOWS

You can create shadow effects to help make objects and images stand out on your slides. Shadow effects are colored duplicates of an object that are placed behind them to appear like shadows. Shadow effects give objects depth and often help differentiate them from their background. For example, if your presentation uses a Design Template and you want to use an image or graphic that is similar in color to the background, it may look like it is fading into the background instead of giving your graphic the visual focus you want.

You can add shadow effects to images, AutoShapes, and even text. You can also choose to use semitransparent shadows that allow the slide's background color to show through the top layer.

When your presentation uses a Design Template, default shadow colors are those used by the Design Template, giving the shadow effects a look that coordinates with the other elements in your presentation. Once you have added a shadow effect, you can reposition the shadow to appear where you want it.

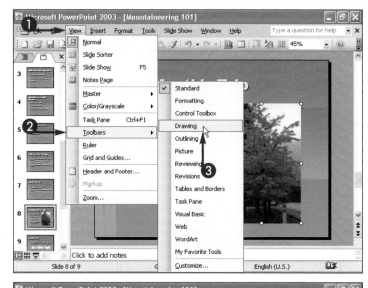

❶ Click View.

❷ Click Toolbars.

❸ Click Drawing.

● The Drawing Toolbar appears.

❹ Click the image or graphic to which you want to apply a shadow.

❺ Click the Shadow Style button.

❻ Click the shadow you want to use.

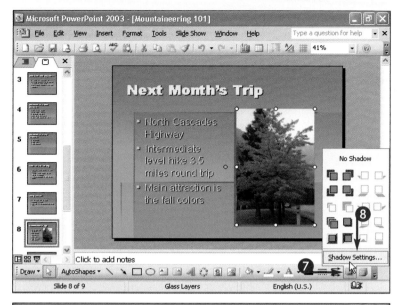

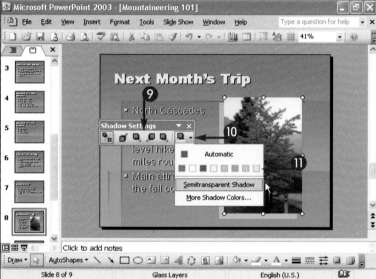

The default shadow is applied.

7 Click the Shadow Style button.

8 Click Shadow Settings.

The Shadow Settings dialog box appears.

9 Click the Nudge buttons to move the shadow up, down, left, or right.

10 Click the Shadow Color ⊡.

11 Click the color you want to use.

The color you select is applied.

TIPS

Caution!
You should use care when you add semitransparent shadow effects. Because the background color shows through, sometimes results can be unexpected. For example, if your slide background color is yellow and you add a semitransparent blue shadow effect, it will appear as a green shadow. The yellow and blue blend together to yield green.

Did You Know?
You can apply a shadow to text by clicking Format and then Font to open the Font dialog box. However, when you use the steps in this task instead, you are able to nudge and resize the shadows.

Did You Know?
You can use the Format Painter to apply your new shadow effect to other objects. For more information about using the Format Painter, see Task #28.

CREATE A LINK
to go elsewhere in the presentation

You can quickly navigate to a specific slide in your presentation with a click of your mouse. PowerPoint automatically creates a bookmark, or a targeted place to link to in your presentation, based on the presentation's outline. Bookmarks are created for each slide in your presentation. You can easily identify which slide to link to because each slide is listed by a slide number and by a slide title. When you create a hyperlink that links to another place in your presentation, you are also creating a hyperlink to a bookmark in the presentation.

Hyperlinks to different parts of your presentation work when you deliver your presentation in Slide Show Mode. By default, they appear on-screen as underlined text, and when you click them, the linked slide automatically appears. Hyperlinks to other locations in your presentations can be particularly convenient when you anticipate questions at specific points in the presentation. You can click the hyperlink to quickly shift to the other slide to help answer those questions.

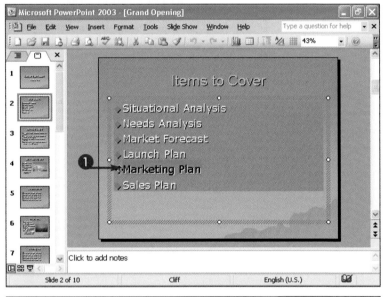

① Click and drag to highlight the text to which you want to add a hyperlink.

② Click Insert.

③ Click Hyperlink.

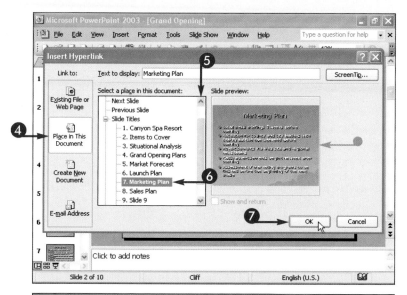

The Insert Hyperlink dialog box appears.

④ Click Place in This Document in the Link to section.

⑤ In the Select a place in this document section, scroll to locate the slide to which you want to link.

⑥ Click the slide.

● A preview of the slide appears in the Slide preview section.

⑦ Click OK.

The hyperlink is added to the slide.

⑧ Press F5 to display the slide in Slide Show Mode.

● You can click the active hyperlink to move throughout your document.

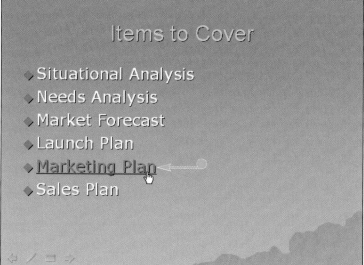

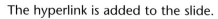

TIPS

Did You Know?
You can link graphics and AutoShapes to other parts of your presentation. Click the object you want to link and then follow steps **2** to **8** above.

Apply It!
You can also create a hyperlink to the previous or next slide. Follow the steps in this task, but in step **6**, click Next Slide or Previous Slide instead of clicking a specific slide.

Apply It!
You can assign a screen tip to each hyperlink. Screen tips are text that appears when you hover over a hyperlink. Follow steps **1** to **6** above and then click Screen Tip. Type the screen tip you want to use, click OK, and then follow steps **7** and **8**.

OPEN A DOCUMENT
with the click of a button

You can open a file in a separate program without leaving PowerPoint when you create an Action Button. Action Buttons are graphical buttons that you can draw onto a slide. You can assign actions to the buttons to perform key tasks. When you create an Action Button that opens a program, it allows you to stay in Slide Show Mode while the other program opens instead of exiting Slide Show Mode, minimizing PowerPoint, and then starting the other program.

Action Buttons are convenient because you can create them from within PowerPoint; it is not necessary to use a separate graphics creation tool to create great-looking buttons. You can create them to be as large or as small as you want.

When you give your presentation, simply click the button and the program opens with the file you specified. Action Buttons that open files can be very useful when you want to be able to refer to a document quickly if needed, such as a brochure, a contract, or a data sheet.

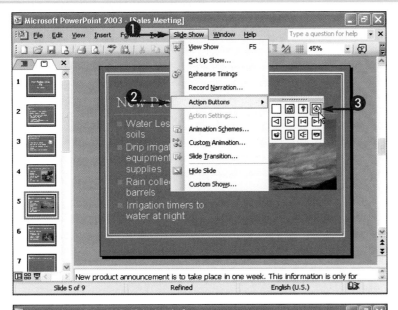

① Click Slide Show.

② Click Action Buttons.

③ Click the Information action button (⌖ changes to +).

④ Click and drag to indicate a size for the action button.

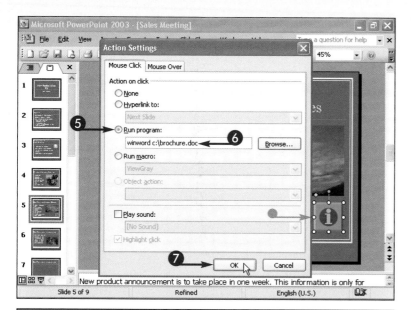

- When you release your mouse, the action button is drawn at the size specified and the Action Settings dialog box appears.

⑤ Click the Run program option (○ changes to ⦿).

⑥ In the Run program field, type the shortcut for the program followed by the file path.

For example, you could open a Word document called brochure.doc by typing **winword c:\brochure.doc** *in the Run program field.*

⑦ Click OK.

The action button is created with a link to open the program and the specific document.

⑧ Press F5 to view the presentation in Slide Show Mode.

- You can click the button on the slide to open a document.

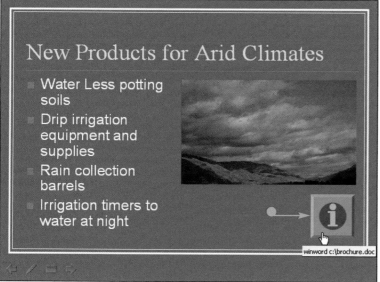

TIPS

Did You Know?

You can open a different program. Find the path to the program by clicking Start and then All Programs. Right-click the program you want to locate and then click Properties. The path is listed in the Target field. You can copy it and paste it into the Run program field in step **6** above. Do not include the quotation marks.

Try This!

This task illustrates how to open a program with a specific file. If you simply want to open the program, follow the steps in this task, but in step **6**, type **winword** in the Run program field.

ADD MOTION
to illustrate your content

You can add motion paths to graphics to draw attention to your content and help illustrate key points in your PowerPoint presentations. Motion paths allow you to bring normal text or graphics onto your slide in linear, curved, or free-form shapes. When you deliver your presentation, the images enter the screen in the path or shape you have chosen.

Adding motion to graphics is a great way to focus attention on an important logo or graphic because the eye is naturally drawn to movement. It is also a

good way to create effects like those produced with Macromedia Flash without using a separate tool or learning a separate program.

You can also apply more than one motion path to an image, each starting after you click your mouse. For example, you could have one part of a diagram slide into place, discuss it, and then click your mouse for the next part of the diagram to slide in, using the motion path you specified.

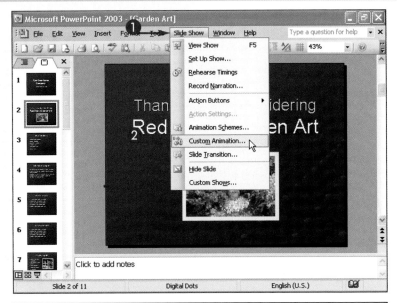

① Click Slide Show.

② Click Custom Animation.

The Custom Animation Task Pane appears.

③ Click Add Effect.

④ Click Motion Paths.

⑤ Click Draw Custom Path.

⑥ Click Curve.

The ⌖ changes to ⌖.

⑦ Click where you want the image to start and then click where you want the image to curve.

⑧ Repeat step **7** until the path is the desired shape.

⑨ Double-click at the end of the motion path.

● The motion path appears on the screen and the action is listed in the Custom Path section of the Custom Animation Task Pane.

⑩ Click here and select the speed you want to use.

⑪ Click Play.

The animation plays for you in the Custom Animation Task Pane.

TIPS

Did You Know?

You can choose to start motion paths one after another instead of waiting for a click before the effect begins. After step **7** above, click the Start ⏷ and select After Previous, then continue with step **9**.

Did You Know?

From within the Custom Animation Task Pane, you can change the length of time it takes for an effect to take place. Follow steps **1** to **11** above; then click and drag the right edge of the box next to the effect to the right to extend the duration of the effect, or click and drag the left edge of the box to the right to shorten the duration.

Make an entrance with CUSTOM ANIMATIONS

You can help illustrate important points better when you create builds out of graphics and text. *Builds* allow you to bring one element into a slide, discuss it, and then click when you are ready for the next element to enter. This is particularly useful when presenting diagrams that have multiple parts, each requiring explanation.

One of the great parts about using builds is that it is not necessary to create a separate slide for each part of the build; all of the build elements make up a single slide. When printed, the slide looks like the results of all the builds.

You can choose from among many entrance styles for each effect. Each entrance style gives the effect a completely different look. You can continue to add entrance effects to each element on the slide until each element appears when desired.

The Custom Animation Task Pane also makes it easy to preview the effects as you build them. When you click the Play button, the Custom Animation plays without entering Slide Show Mode.

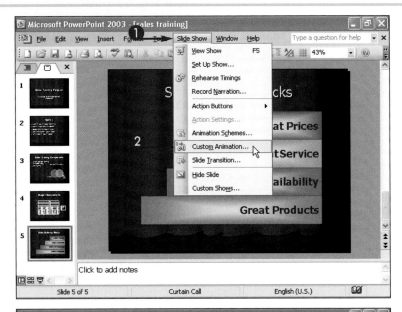

① Click Slide Show.

② Click Custom Animation.

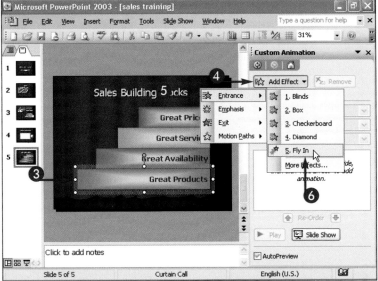

The Custom Animation Task Pane appears.

③ Click the item on which you want to apply the effect.

④ Click Add Effect.

⑤ Click Entrance.

⑥ Click Fly In.

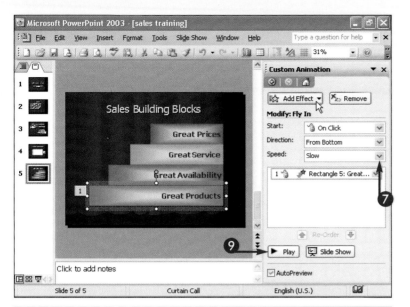

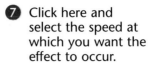

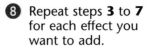

The effect is added in the Custom Animation Task Pane.

⑦ Click here and select the speed at which you want the effect to occur.

⑧ Repeat steps **3** to **7** for each effect you want to add.

⑨ Click Play.

The animation plays for you.

TIPS

Important!

It is usually easier to first create your slide with all text and graphics placed where desired, and then go back and create the build effects. This ensures that all of the slide elements fit together when the builds have completed.

Try This!

You can also create entrance effects that occur one after another instead of occurring only after you click your mouse. Follow steps **1** to **6** above and then click the Start ▾. Click After Previous and then follow steps **7** to **9** above.

Change It!

You can change the direction in which the effects appear. Follow steps **1** to **6**, click the Direction ▾, and then click the direction you want to use.

Orchestrate an exit with
CUSTOM ANIMATIONS

You can create impressive presentations when you use builds to have text or graphics exit from your slide by clicking your mouse. Using exit effects can help viewers focus on topics that are currently being discussed as the contents are removed.

You can also use exit effects to generate excitement on slides. For example, you can use a combination of entrance and exit effects to display and then remove customer quotes or positive feedback to help give your slide visual impact and a feeling of excitement about the products or services being discussed.

If you use exit effects frequently, you can change effect styles for variety. For example, one image could exit using the Checkerboard style, and one text area could exit using the Diamond style.

By default, exit effects occur at high speed. However, you can set exit effects to take place more slowly for a more subtle style. You can create multiple exit effects on each slide, and after each build, you can preview your exit effects from within the Custom Animation Task Pane.

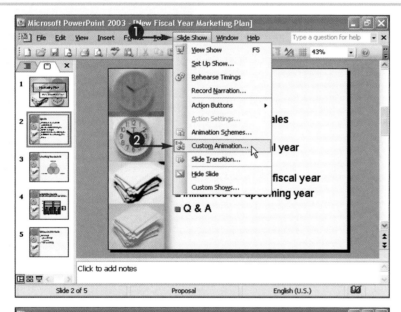

① Click Slide Show.

② Click Custom Animation.

The Custom Animation Task Pane appears.

③ Highlight the text on which you want to place an effect.

④ Click Add Effect.

⑤ Click Exit.

⑥ Click the effect you want to apply.

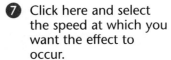

The effect is added in the Custom Animation Task Pane.

⑦ Click here and select the speed at which you want the effect to occur.

⑧ Repeat steps **3** to **7** for each effect you want to apply on the slide.

⑨ Click Play.

The animation plays for you.

TIPS

Change It!

You can change the order in which exit effects take place. After following the steps above, click the effect you want to reorder, and then click the Re-Order ⬆ or ⬇ until the effect is in the desired order.

Did You Know?

Exit effects can occur one after another instead of after you click your mouse. Follow steps **1** to **6**; then click the Start ⬇ and select After Previous. Then follow steps **7** to **9**.

Did You Know?

You can change the direction in which an effect exits the screen. Follow steps **1** to **6** above; then click the Direction ⬇ and select the direction you want to use. Then follow steps **7** to **9**.

Choreograph effects to make a
MULTIMEDIA PRESENTATION

You can create visually interesting presentations that help you tell a story when you choreograph effects. Choreographed effects can have different start or stop times and can include entrance effects, exit effects, motion paths, or even audio or video.

For example, if you want to illustrate a timeline of events, you could bring in a graphic, discuss it, and then bring in another graphic as the one you just discussed exits the screen. When you want to discuss complex topics, choreographing effects can help you

break them down into pieces that are easier to understand.

After each effect is created, it is listed in the Custom Animation Task Pane, where you can determine whether the effect begins with a mouse click or whether it begins after the previous effect is completed. This is very useful when you want to illustrate how pieces fit together by displaying one piece, then another immediately thereafter. You can choose the speed at which effects occur.

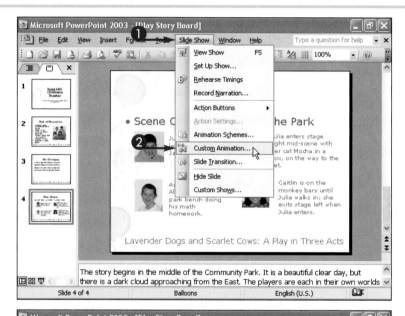

① Click Slide Show.

② Click Custom Animation.

The Custom Animation Task Pane appears.

③ Click the object on which you want to apply an entrance effect.

④ Click Add Effect.

⑤ Click Entrance.

⑥ Click the effect you want to apply.

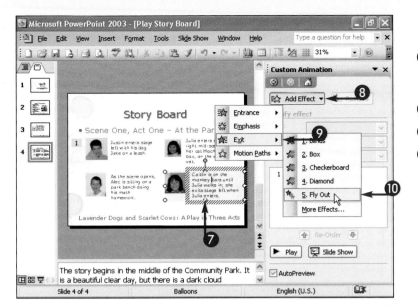

The effect is added to the object.

⑦ Click the object to which you want to add an exit effect.

⑧ Click Add Effect.

⑨ Click Exit.

⑩ Click the effect you want to apply.

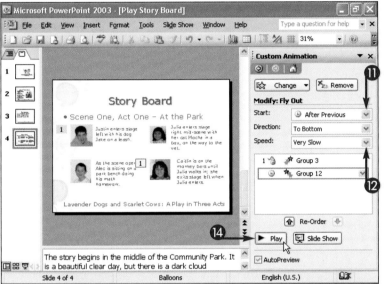

The exit effect is added to the object.

⑪ Click here and select After Previous from the Start menu.

⑫ Click here and select a speed from the Speed menu.

⑬ Repeat steps **3** to **12** for each object on which you want to apply an effect.

⑭ Click Play.

The animation plays your arranged effects.

TIPS

Did You Know?

If you have more than one element that you would like to enter or exit at the same time, you can group the elements first, and then apply the effect. Simply press Ctrl+click to select items such as text or graphics, and then follow the steps above.

Try This!

You can orchestrate effects so that they occur at the same time. Follow the steps above, but in step **11**, click With Previous instead of After Previous.

Re-Order!

You can change the order in which exit effects take place. After following the steps above, click the effect to reorder and then click the Re-Order ⬆ or ⬇ to move the effect to its desired position.

Give your presentation a professional look with
TRANSITION EFFECTS

You can give your presentations a more polished look when you apply transition effects between your slides. Transition effects determine what happens between the time you click your mouse to advance to the next slide and the time the next slide loads.

By default, presentations do not use transition effects. However, PowerPoint gives you many professional-looking transition effects you can apply to your slides. For example, the Dissolve effect removes blocks of your slide and then rebuilds it with the next slide.

When you apply a transition effect, you can see how it will look from within the Slide Transition Task Pane. This saves time because it is not necessary to view your presentation in Slide Show Mode in order to see how the effect will look.

Once you apply the transition effect to your slides, you can adjust the speed at which it occurs, and you can even include sound effects. For example, you can apply the Drum Roll sound effect before an announcement slide or the Applause sound effect before a congratulatory slide.

① Click Slide Show.

② Click Slide Transition.

The Slide Transition Task Pane appears.

③ In the Apply to selected slides section, click a transition effect.

A preview of the transition appears on the slide.

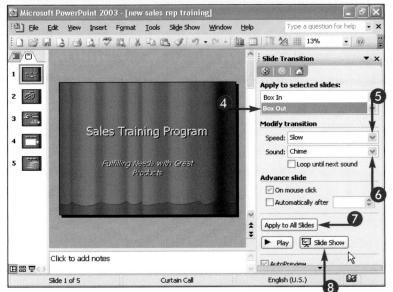

43

DIFFICULTY LEVEL

④ In the Apply to selected slides section, click the transition effect you want to use.

⑤ Click here and select the speed at which you want the transition to appear.

⑥ Click here and select the sound effect you want to play while the transition is occurring.

⑦ Click Apply to All Slides.

⑧ Click Slide Show.

The presentation plays in Slide Show Mode with the desired transitions.

TIPS

Try This!
You can apply different transition effects to each slide. Simply omit step **7** above and then repeat the steps for each slide to which you want to apply a transition effect, omitting step **7** each time.

Automate It!
If you want to automate your presentation to advance each slide after a predetermined number of seconds, follow steps **1** to **6**, and then in step **7**, click the Automatically after option (☐ changes to ☑). Click the Automatically after ⬍ to select the number of seconds at which you want the slide to advance to the next one, and then follow steps **7** and **8**.

Add interest with
ANIMATION SCHEMES

You can quickly and easily add movement to your slides by applying an Animation Scheme. Animation Schemes are preconfigured combinations of effects that you would normally have to apply individually. Animation Schemes can include entrance effects, exit effects, transition effects, motion paths, and more.

For example, if you apply the Unfold Animation Scheme, the slides wipe onto the screen using a transition effect, the title falls into place letter by letter, the subtitle appears as a slow wipe from the left, bulleted lists enter one by one and letter by

letter from the left, and more. It would take some time to create Custom Animations to replicate these effects, which makes Animation Schemes even more appealing; they are easy to apply, and they greatly enhance your presentation's look and function.

PowerPoint makes it easy to decide which Animation Scheme to use. You can view how the Animation Scheme will affect your slide from within the Slide Design Task Pane. Animation Schemes are also conveniently divided into three categories: Subtle, Moderate, and Exciting.

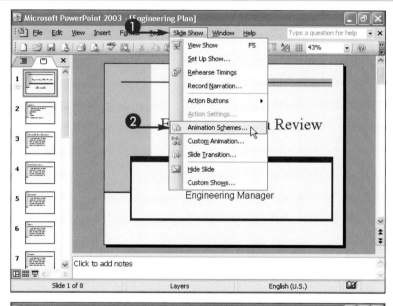

① Click Slide Show.

② Click Animation Schemes.

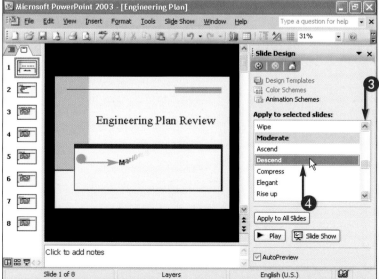

The Slide Design Task Pane appears.

③ In the Apply to selected slides section, scroll up or down to locate your scheme.

④ Click an animation scheme you want to apply to the slide.

● The effect is previewed on the slide.

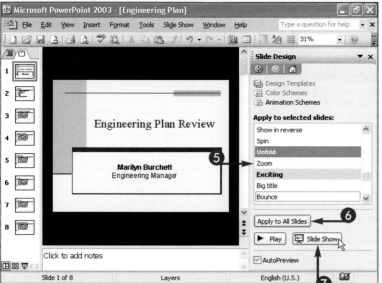

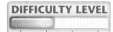

5 Repeat step **3** to experiment with different schemes before applying your selection.

6 Click Apply to All Slides.

7 Click Slide Show.

DIFFICULTY LEVEL

The presentation opens in Slide Show Mode with the Animation Scheme applied.

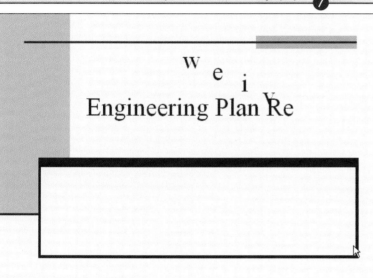

TIPS

Did You Know?

When you use Animation Schemes, they often apply effects to bulleted lists that bring in a new bullet after each click. Trying to quickly advance to another slide in the presentation may mean a lot of clicking. To get to another slide faster while in Slide Show Mode, simply type the slide number and then press Enter.

Did You Know?

When you apply an Animation Scheme to all slides, even new slides that you create will use this Animation Scheme.

Remove It!

If you have applied an Animation Scheme that you no longer want to use, follow the steps above. In step **5**, click No Animation.

Communicate with Audio and Video

You can enhance your presentations with audio and video to improve communication. Audio and video can come from a variety of sources, such as recordings from previous presentations, audio and video from the Clip Art Gallery, and even CDs.

You can play audio and video clips in a separate player, or you can embed the player into your slide so that the audio or video clip looks like it is part of the slide. Because Microsoft Windows Media Player comes with PowerPoint, it is the player used in this chapter.

The key to getting audio and video to play or record properly in PowerPoint is to first get the audio to play or record properly outside

PowerPoint. Once your audio/video capabilities are set up on your computer, you can use PowerPoint to record the audio for your presentation and automatically match that audio with each slide so that your viewers can listen to your audio at the same time they view your presentation.

If you want an audio or video clip to play only when you are ready for it, you can create a button that plays a clip when clicked. You can also play a sound when you hover your mouse over an object, or you can loop audio so it repeats indefinitely. You can also choreograph multiple sound or video effects on a slide to produce a professional presentation that gets your work noticed.

Top 100

ADD A BUTTON
to play your video clip

You can add a button to your slide that, when clicked, plays a video clip. This is a great way to play video clips only when you are ready for them. For example, if you are delivering a presentation about an event and you are not sure if you will have time to play your video clip, you can insert a button onto the slide that plays the video only when it is clicked.

The created button is an Action Button. Action Buttons make it easy to create a button of any size, and then assign an action to the button that takes

place when the button is clicked. In this case, the action is to open the Windows Media Player with a specific video clip.

In order to launch the player, you will need to know the name of the file that is executed to open that program, such as mplayer2.exe for the older Windows Media Player, or wmplayer.exe for the newer Windows Media Player. You will also need to know the path to the file you want the player to open.

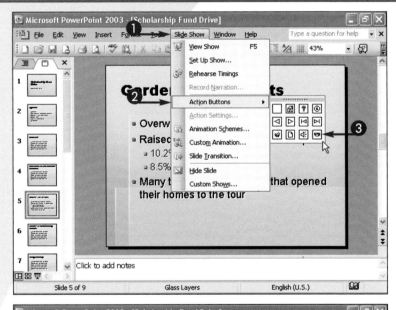

① Click Slide Show.

② Click Action Buttons.

③ Click Movie action button
(⬚ changes to +).

④ Click and drag where you want to position the button.

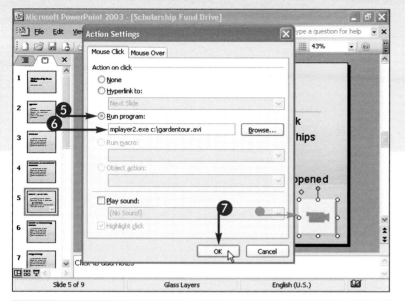

Garden Tour Results

● The button is created, and the Action Settings dialog box appears.

 # 45

DIFFICULTY LEVEL

⑤ Click the Run program option (○ changes to ◉).

⑥ Type **mplayer2.exe** and a space, followed by the path to your video file, for example, **c:\gardentour.avi**, in the Run program field.

⑦ Click OK.

The play video action is now assigned to the button.

⑧ Press F5 to open the presentation in Slide Show Mode.

The presentation opens in Slide Show Mode.

⑨ Click the video button.

The video plays.

TIPS

Did You Know?

You can also browse to the program you want to open instead of typing the name. After step **5**, click Browse. On the Select a Program to Run dialog box, click the Look in ☑, and then click the folder in which the program resides. Click the program, and then click OK. Then proceed with step **7**.

Try This!

You can use a different player program. Substitute the player program name in step **6**. You can find the path to a program by clicking Start, All Programs, and then right-clicking the program for which you want to find the path. Click Properties and then click the General tab. The location is displayed in the Location field.

EMBED VIDEO

to turn your slide into a movie

You can use video clips in your presentations to help tell a story. Video delivers more impact when it is integrated into your slide. For example, if your presentation is designed to train viewers on a particular topic, you can incorporate the Windows Media Player into your slide to allow them to see the video, stop it, adjust the volume, mute it, and more. You can also make the video even more useful when you add a bulleted list of text next to it to highlight key points. When you embed the player into your

slide, you are given more control over positioning and the ability to see other content as well as the video at the same time.

When you insert the Windows Media Player Object into your slide, its properties are fully editable. You can edit the Windows Media Player Object properties to instruct the player what file to play. You will need to know the path to the file to be played in order for the video to play successfully.

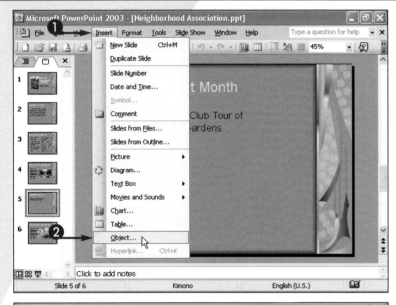

① Click Insert.

② Click Object.

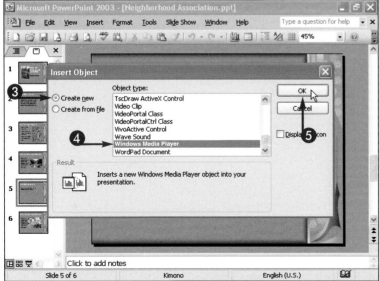

The Insert Object dialog box appears.

③ Click the Create new option (○ changes to ⊙).

④ In the Object type section, scroll down and click Windows Media Player.

⑤ Click OK.

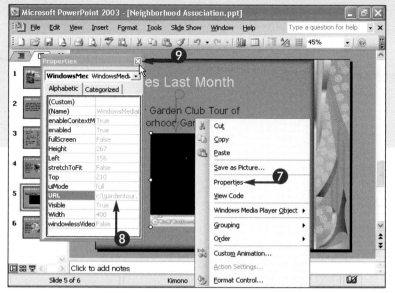

● The Windows Media Player control is inserted onto the slide.

6 Right-click the control to open the content menu.

7 Click Properties to open its dialog box.

8 In the URL field, type the path to your video file.

9 Click ⊠.

The Windows Media Player is configured to play your video file.

10 Press F5 to view your presentation in Slide Show Mode.

The presentation plays in Slide Show Mode with the video displaying in the Windows Media Player on the slide.

Did You Know?

The Windows Media Player Object does not automatically adjust its size to the size of your video, so it could be too small or too large for your content. You should know the dimensions of your video (height and width) in pixels and edit the Windows Media Player Object properties to match those dimensions. To do so, follow steps **1** to **8** above, and then type your video's width in the Width field and your video's height in the Height field. Then proceed with step **9**.

Change It!

Once the Windows Media Player Object has been inserted into the slide, you can still edit its properties, such as the display size or types of controls displayed. Right-click the Windows Media Player Object and then click Properties.

ADD SOUND
from a file

You can make your presentations more interesting by adding audio clips that contain entertaining or informative content. For example, if you are holding a conference and want to display a welcome slide in the front of the room while attendees get settled, you can add an audio clip that plays music while the slide is on the screen. Additionally, if you are presenting a slide that discusses how happy customers are with your product, you can insert directly into the slide an audio clip of a customer talking about your product to really emphasize your points.

When you insert an audio clip from a file, a small audio icon is placed onto the slide. That audio icon can be clicked and dragged to the desired location on the screen. When you are ready for the audio clip to play while you are in Slide Show Mode, you simply click the audio icon and the audio plays. The audio clip does not play in an external media player; it plays through your computer's audio system.

① Click Insert.

② Click Movies and Sounds.

③ Click Sound from File.

The Insert Sound dialog box appears.

④ Click here and select the folder in which the audio file you want to play is located.

⑤ Click the file you want to play.

⑥ Click OK.

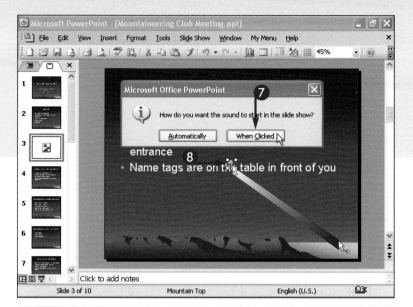

The Microsoft Office PowerPoint dialog box appears.

DIFFICULTY LEVEL

⑦ Click When Clicked.

The audio symbol is inserted into the slide.

⑧ Click and drag the audio symbol to where you want it to appear on the slide.

⑨ Press F5 to open the presentation in Slide Show Mode.

The presentation plays in Slide Show Mode.

⑩ Click the audio symbol.

The audio plays.

Welcome!
Mountaineering Club Monthly Meeting

- Refreshments are at the back table
- Please sign in; the clipboard is at the entrance
- Name tags are on the table in front of you

 TIPS

Did You Know?
You can choose to make your audio begin playing automatically instead of starting the audio with a mouse click. Follow the steps above, but in step **7**, click Automatically instead of When Clicked. However, with this option, you cannot click 🔊 to stop the audio when in Slide Show Mode.

More Options!
If you want to listen to the audio while you are still in Normal View in PowerPoint, simply double-click 🔊. To stop it, click 🔊 again.

Try This!
The audio plays using the volume settings set in the Sounds and Audio Devices program. To access Sounds and Audio Devices, click Start, Control Panel, and then double-click Sounds and Audio Devices.

Play on and on with
LOOPED AUDIO

You can use looped audio to play music or a message repeatedly in your presentations. Looped audio is repeated from beginning to end until it is interrupted. Looped audio can be particularly useful in presentations where you cannot predict how long a viewer will stay on one slide. For example, if you plan to display a slide during a break in a conference, you may want to play music or an instructional message for the duration of the break. Adding a

looped audio file to the slide will allow you to walk away from the presentation assured that the audio will continue to play until you are ready to begin again.

Adding looped audio to a slide is like adding an audio clip from a file to the slide. After the audio clip is added to the slide, you can edit the Sound Object's properties to instruct the clip to play in a loop.

① Click Insert.

② Click Movies and Sounds.

③ Click Sound from File.

The Insert Sound dialog box appears.

④ Click here and select the folder in which the audio file is located.

⑤ Click the audio file you want to play.

⑥ Click OK.

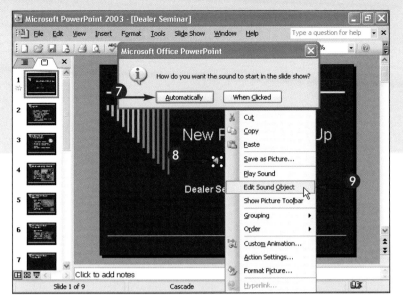

The Microsoft Office PowerPoint dialog box appears.

⑦ Click Automatically.

A symbol representing your audio file () appears on the slide.

⑧ Right-click the audio symbol.

The content menu appears.

⑨ Click Edit Sound Object.

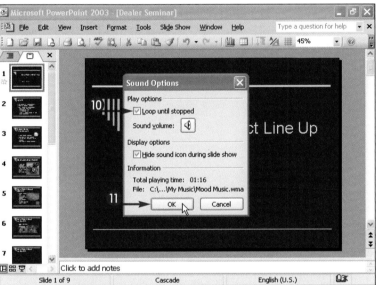

The Sound Options dialog box appears.

⑩ Click the Loop until stopped option (☐ changes to ☑).

⑪ Click OK.

The looped audio is set to play in your presentation.

TIPS

Try This!
You can easily move by clicking and dragging it to the desired position on the slide.

Apply It!
You can choose to start the looped audio only after is clicked. Follow the steps above, but in step **7**, click When Clicked instead of Automatically.

Did You Know?
You can change the volume at which the audio clip plays. To change the volume, after step **9** above, click the Sound Volume button (🔊). Use the slider bar to increase or decrease the volume, click the Sound Options dialog box, and then proceed to step **10**.

Boost your presentation with
AUDIO FROM A CD

You can enhance your presentation with audio and save time when you play audio directly from a CD. It is not necessary to upload music to your computer's hard drive in order to play it from PowerPoint. Instead, you can instruct PowerPoint to play audio directly from the CD player in your computer.

For example, if you want to play music from a CD before and after a seminar, and during breaks, you can insert audio into introductory, break, and conclusion slides to play directly from a CD. You can even specify exactly what tracks on the CD you want to play.

You can also choose to loop audio to play repeatedly until it is interrupted. For example, you could choose to continually play tracks 1 through 4 of a CD until interrupted during a break. The audio can be interrupted when you click to advance to the next slide.

When you deliver your presentation, a CD symbol is inserted into the slide that can be clicked to start playing the audio again from the beginning.

1 Click Insert.

2 Click Movies and Sounds.

3 Click Play CD Audio Track.

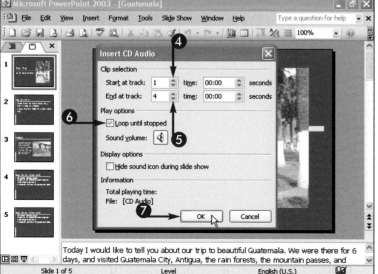

The Insert CD Audio dialog box appears.

4 In the Start at track section, click to select the track number at which you want to start.

5 In the End at track section, click to select the track number at which you want to end.

6 Click the Loop until stopped option (☐ changes to ☑).

7 Click OK.

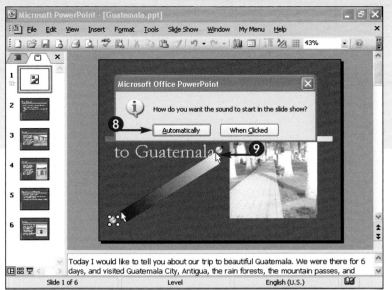

The Microsoft Office PowerPoint dialog box appears.

⑧ Click Automatically.

The CD audio symbol () is inserted onto the slide.

⑨ Click and drag the CD audio symbol to where you want it on the slide.

⑩ Press F5 to view your presentation in Slide Show Mode.

DIFFICULTY LEVEL

The presentation opens in Slide Show Mode and the audio plays from CD.

Our Trip
to Guatemala

TIPS

Caution!
When you deliver your presentation, PowerPoint plays audio from whatever CD is in your computer's CD player. If you design your presentation with one CD in mind, but the CD player has another CD in it when you deliver your presentation, you could get unexpected results.

Caution!
You should make sure that the license agreement that came with your CD allows you to play the music in public forums.

Did You Know?
You can play only a selected part of an audio track. After step **4**, click the Time control 🔼 to set the start time. After step **5**, click the Time control 🔼 to set the stop time.

INSERT AN AUDIO BUTTON
in your slide

You can add depth to your presentations when you insert audio clips into your slides. You can make the effects look even more professional when you create buttons that link to audio clips.

Placing a button on a slide with an audio symbol makes it more obvious to presenters or viewers that supplemental audio is available for a slide. For example, when you place an audio clip onto a slide, a very small audio symbol is normally inserted. It is small enough that it could be missed by the

presenter and the viewer. When you create an audio button, it draws attention to the fact that there is an audio clip available for the slide.

Audio buttons are added to the slide by creating an Action Button, which is a professional-looking image that you can draw onto your slide in whatever size you want. They are called Action Buttons because you can assign actions that make them interactive, such as linking to an audio file when the button is clicked.

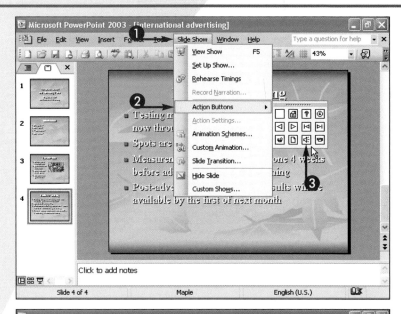

1 Click Slide Show.

2 Click Action Buttons.

3 Click the Sound action button
(⌖ changes to +).

4 Click and drag where you want to position the button.

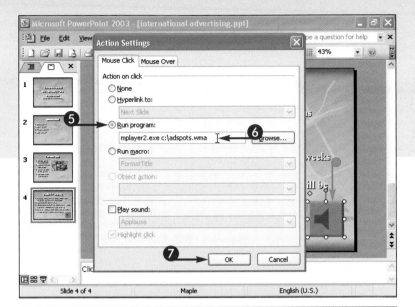

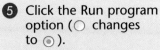

- The button is created, and the Action Settings dialog box appears.

5 Click the Run program option (○ changes to ⦿).

6 Type **mplayer2.exe** followed by the path to your video, for example, **c:\adspots.wma**, in the Run program field.

7 Click OK.

The play audio action is now assigned to the button.

8 Press F5 to open the presentation in Slide Show Mode.

The presentation opens in Slide Show Mode.

9 Click the audio button.

The audio plays.

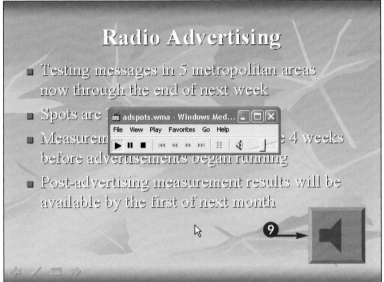

TIPS

Try This!
The easiest way to test and see whether an Action Button will work is to try typing the text in step **6** in the Windows Run dialog box. If it works from the Run dialog box, chances are that it will work from an Action Button. Click Start, Run, and then in the Run dialog box, type the code in step **6** in the Open field.

Customize It!
If you want to use a player other than Windows Media Player to play the audio, in step **6**, type the program-path file-path, for example, **wmplayer.exe c:\gardentour.avi**.

Did You Know?
The color of the Action Button is determined by the Design Template you are using on this slide.

Hover your mouse to
PLAY A SOUND

You can add entertainment value to text or images when you add an effect that plays a sound when you hover your mouse over the object. For example, if you have a slide that announces the winners of a skateboarding contest, you can add impact and a festive feeling if viewers hear applause when you hover your mouse over a picture of the winning skateboarders. In the same way, on a slide presenting great photos, you can add the sound of a camera when you hover your mouse over each image.

You can add hover sounds to text or images by using Action Settings. Action Settings allow you to create hyperlinks, run programs, run macros, or apply sound effects like Applause, Arrow, Bomb, Breeze, Camera, Cash Register, and Chime. You can also add more than one effect to an object, such as the launch of a video clip and a sound effect at the same time you hover over an object.

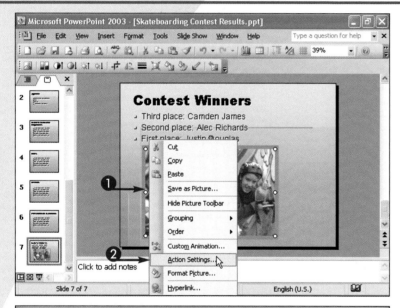

1 Right-click the image to which you want to apply the hover effect.

The content menu appears.

2 Click Action Settings.

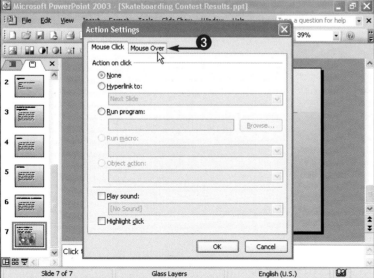

The Action Settings dialog box appears.

3 Click the Mouse Over tab.

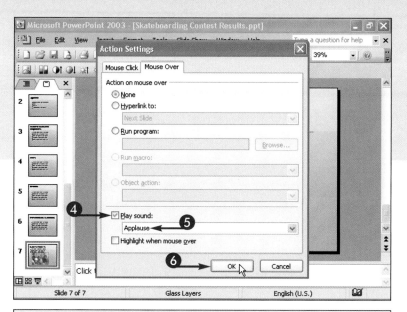

④ Click the Play sound option (☐ changes to ☑).

⑤ Click here and select the sound you want to use.

⑥ Click OK.

The effect is applied to the image.

⑦ Press F5 to display the presentation in Slide Show Mode.

The presentation plays in Slide Show Mode.

⑧ Position your mouse cursor over the image.

The sound plays.

TIPS

Did You Know?
You can also choose to apply audio effects to run when clicked instead of hovered over. Follow the steps above, but omit step **3**.

Try This!
The hover effect works when you are viewing your presentation in Slide Show Mode.

Did You Know?
Audio effects work when your computer system is properly configured for audio. As a rule, if you can hear system sounds, such as Windows when it starts up, your audio effects will work in PowerPoint.

More Options!
You can also apply sound effects to hyperlinks. First, create the hyperlink and follow the steps above. However, in step **1**, right-click the hyperlink to which you want to apply the sound effect.

RECORD NARRATIONS
for your slides

You can prepare your presentation for use when you are not there by recording narrations for your slides. The Record Narration tool allows you to record audio for your presentation, and afterward, when the presentation is viewed in Slide Show Mode, your audio accompanies the slide.

You can save time by using the Record Narration tool because it not only helps you record the audio for your presentation, it keeps track of the timing for each slide and then automatically advances to the next slide at the appropriate time. For example, if

you want others to be able to view your presentation on their own, you can use Record Narration to record your voice for each slide, synchronized to advance to the next slide at just the right time.

When you choose to link narrations to a location on your hard drive, the audio file for each slide is stored separately on your computer. This keeps the file size down and keeps performance high. If you choose not to link narrations, the audio is stored with the presentation.

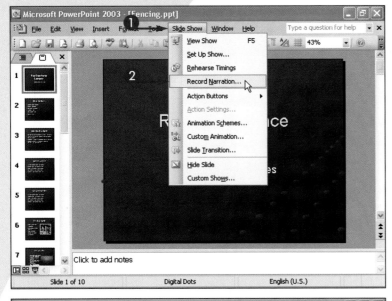

① Click Slide Show.

② Click Record Narration.

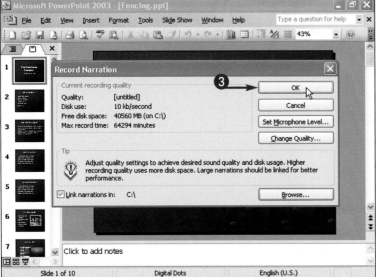

The Record Narration dialog box appears.

③ Click OK.

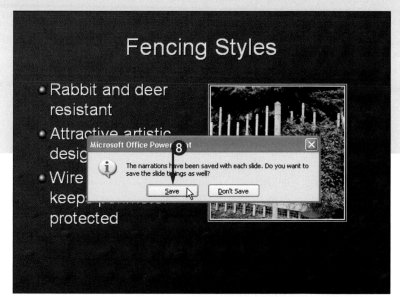

Fencing Styles

- Rabbit and deer resistant
- Attractive artistic design
- Wire keeps perimeter protected

Microsoft Office PowerPoint

The narrations have been saved with each slide. Do you want to save the slide timings as well?

[Save] [Don't Save]

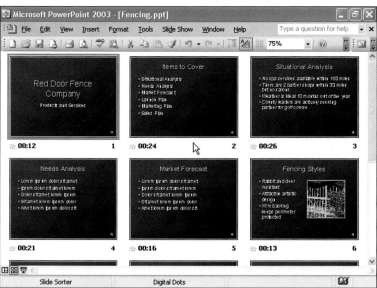

Microsoft PowerPoint 2003 - [Fencing.ppt]

File   Edit   View   Insert   Format   Tools   Slide Show   Window   Help

Type a question for help

75%

Red Door Fence Company

Products and Services

00:12   1

Items to Cover

- Situational Analysis
- Needs Analysis
- Market Forecast
- Launch Plan
- Marketing Plan
- Sales Plan

00:24   2

Situational Analysis

- No spa services available within 150 miles
- There are 2 barber shops within 30 miles but no salons
- Weather is ideal 10 months out of the year
- County leaders are actively seeking partner for golf course

00:26   3

Needs Analysis

- Lorem ipsum dolor sit amet
- Ipsum dolor sit amet lorem
- Dolor sit amet lorem ipsum
- Sit amet lorem ipsum dolor
- Amet lorem ipsum dolor sit

00:21   4

Market Forecast

- Lorem ipsum dolor sit amet
- Ipsum dolor sit amet lorem
- Dolor sit amet lorem ipsum
- Sit amet lorem ipsum dolor
- Amet lorem ipsum dolor sit

00:16   5

Fencing Styles

- Rabbit and deer resistant
- Attractive artistic design
- Wire backing keeps perimeter protected

00:13   6

Slide Sorter   Digital Dots

The presentation opens in Slide Show Mode.

④ Give your presentation while recording audio into your microphone.

⑤ Press the spacebar to advance to the next slide.

⑥ Repeat steps **4** and **5** for all of the slides to which you want to record narrations.

⑦ Press the Esc key when you have finished recording.

The Microsoft Office PowerPoint dialog box appears.

⑧ Click Save.

The presentation is shown in Slide Sorter View with the timings for each narration listed under each slide.

52

DIFFICULTY LEVEL

TIPS

Change It!

Because each person's voice and volume varies, you will need to adjust most microphones to the correct levels before recording. PowerPoint includes tools to optimize recording. To access these tools, before step **3** above, click the Set Microphone Level button in the Record Narration dialog box.

Caution!

You can set quality levels to determine the richness of the audio recording. While everyone wants the best quality possible, high-quality recordings take more hard disk space and make file sizes larger. To adjust levels to give you the best quality for the bandwidth or file size available, before step **3** above, click the Change Quality button in the Record Narration dialog box.

Create a
NARRATED SLIDE SHOW

You can go back and match audio clips with slides in a presentation that has been recorded. Once you match the audio clip with each slide, the audio clip plays automatically when the slide opens.

For example, if one of your company's executives delivers a presentation at a conference where the audio is recorded, you can package that presentation so that viewers can listen to the audio clip from the presentation at the same time they view the slides. This is a great way to deliver training materials, to

circulate the presentation's message broadly, and to leverage existing resources.

First, split the recording of the presentation into separate audio files, where there is one audio file for each slide's audio. Once the audio files are created, each slide is edited to insert the audio clip for that slide. In addition, you can hide the audio symbol when delivering the presentation in Slide Show Mode to keep your slides clean and uncluttered.

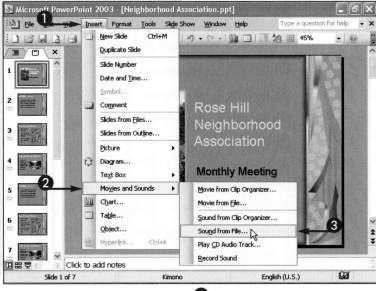

① Click Insert.

② Click Movies and Sounds.

③ Click Sound from File.

The Insert Sound dialog box appears.

④ Click here and select the folder in which the audio clip file is located.

⑤ Click the audio file you want to match to this slide.

⑥ Click OK.

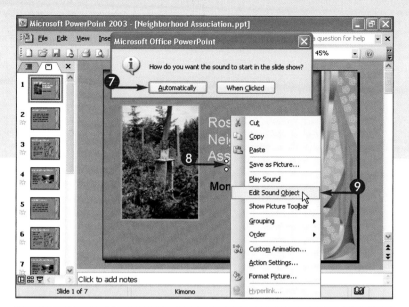

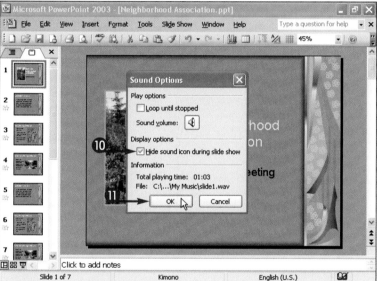

The Microsoft Office PowerPoint dialog box appears.

#53

DIFFICULTY LEVEL

7 Click Automatically.

The audio symbol (🔊) is inserted onto the slide.

8 Right-click the audio symbol.

The content menu appears.

9 Click Edit Sound Object.

The Sound Options dialog box appears.

10 Click the Hide sound icon during slide show option (☐ changes to ☑).

11 Click OK.

12 Repeat steps **1** to **11** for each slide to which you want to add an audio clip.

TIPS

Try This!

You can choose to play the audio when clicked instead of automatically. In step **7** above, click When Clicked instead of Automatically, and then proceed with step **8**. Omit step **10**, or you will not be able to see the audio symbol (🔊) on which to click.

Did You Know?

When you insert audio files into your presentation, they are stored in the presentation itself. When there are many audio files or the audio files are very large, your presentation file size increases. If it becomes too big, you may want to consider using Record Narration instead, because you can link to audio files instead of embedding them in the presentation. See Task #52 for more information about Record Narration.

Produce a professional presentation when you
SYNCHRONIZE EFFECTS

You can use PowerPoint to produce a professional multimedia presentation. Multimedia presentations include audio, video, and effects. PowerPoint can help you synchronize all of them to play when and where you want.

For example, a slide can contain a transition effect, an audio file to play when the slide is loaded, and an entrance effect on a graphic to make it enter slowly at a small size and then expand to its normal size. You can coordinate each of these effects to play at just the right time and for the desired duration.

You can use the Custom Animation Task Pane to reorder effects and change the speed at which they occur. You can also use the timeline to click and drag fields representing the beginning and end times for an effect to move them where you want in a graphical and easy-to-use fashion. Additionally, you can set effects to occur simultaneously with the previous effect, after the previous effect is finished, or upon clicking the mouse.

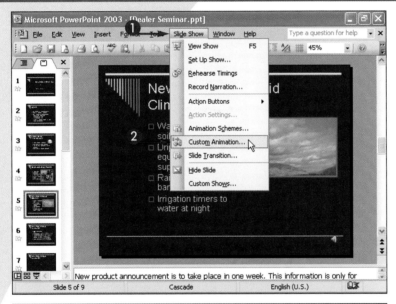

① Click Slide Show.

② Click Custom Animation.

The Custom Animation Task Pane appears.

③ Click an effect of which you want to change preferences.

④ Click here and select After Previous.

⑤ Click the Re-Order ⬆ or ⬇ until the effect is in the desired order.

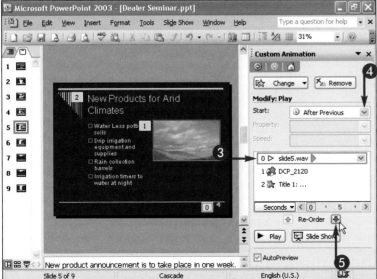

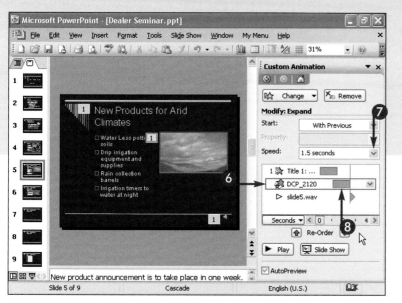

6 Click an effect of which you want to change preferences.

7 Click here and select the speed.

8 Click the field that represents the effect you want to move, and then drag it to the desired position on the timeline.

9 Click the left or right margin of the field that represents the duration of an effect that you want to extend or contract, and then drag it to extend or contract the duration.

10 Click Slide Show.

The presentation plays in Slide Show Mode with the effects in the desired order and with the specified preferences.

TIPS

Caution!

Because audio files have a fixed duration, you cannot click and drag the end point of an audio file displayed in the Custom Animation Task Pane to extend its play. Instead, you can loop the audio to make it repeat. For more information about looping audio, see Task #48.

Apply It!

When you click the Play button on the Custom Animation Task Pane, you can see a preview of all of the effects on the slide.

Did You Know?

Animation Schemes are another great way to create a multimedia presentation. They include preset transitions, entrance and exit effects, motion paths, and more. For more information about Animation Schemes, see Task #44.

Enhance Your Presentations with Custom Content

You can communicate more effectively when you use specialized content to illustrate important information or concepts. You can include hyperlinks to Web pages in your presentations to bring in information and resources on demand to answer questions that arise. You can even include hyperlinks to e-mail addresses so that potential customers can easily reach you.

The Equation Editor can make fast work out of typing and formatting equations. You can also insert symbols to represent characters that are not on your keyboard, such as ®, ©, or even ™.

If you work with financial or statistical data, you can put it to good use by inserting it into your slide from a Microsoft Excel spreadsheet.

You can even insert Excel functionality into your presentation if you want to display data that requires calculations. You can also graphically communicate numerical data in your slides by inserting an Excel-based chart.

You can use diagrams more effectively when you connect AutoShapes to form lines or arrows between objects. These lines stay connected even when you move the objects. You can also use the Organization Chart to update your organizational changes.

If you use a Tablet PC to create or edit your presentations, you can use Ink Annotations to make free-form notes or sketches directly onto your slides.

Top 100

LINK TO THE WEB
from your presentations

You can create hyperlinks to pages or sites on the World Wide Web to supplement the content in your presentations. These links are available to click when you deliver your presentation in Slide Show Mode. The hyperlinks are underlined so that you can differentiate them from normal text. When you click the link, your Internet browser opens with the Web page loaded.

You can also create hyperlinks to pages on your company's intranet site. For example, in a presentation about company sales performance, you

can include links to supplemental sales data in case detailed questions are asked about the points in your slides. Likewise, when giving a presentation about your company's marketing efforts, you can include a link to your company's Web site and internal marketing sites.

You can also add hyperlinks to graphics, AutoShapes, or other objects on your slides. To create a hyperlink on a graphic or AutoShape, follow the steps below, but in step **1**, click the graphic or AutoShape, and then proceed with step **2**.

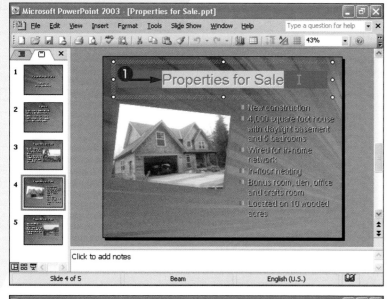

① Highlight the text to which you want to add the hyperlink.

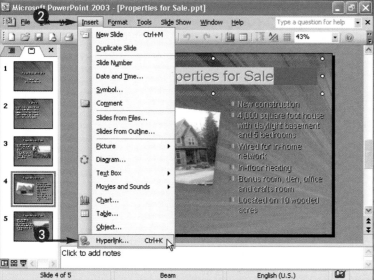

② Click Insert.

③ Click Hyperlink.

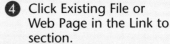

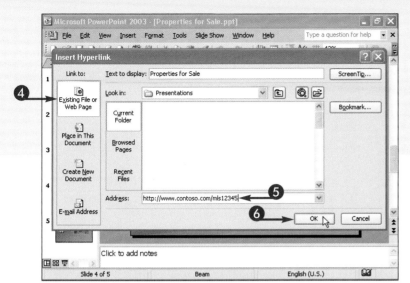

The Insert Hyperlink dialog box appears.

④ Click Existing File or Web Page in the Link to section.

⑤ Type the address for the Web page you want to link to in the Address field.

⑥ Click OK.

The Insert Hyperlink dialog box closes.

⑦ Press F5 to view the slide in Slide Show Mode.

● The slide appears in Slide Show Mode with the hyperlink.

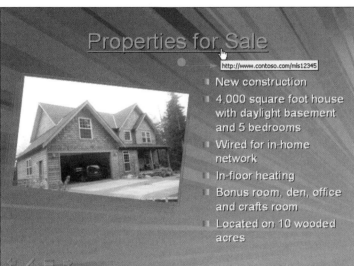

TIPS

Change It!

By default, when you hover your mouse over the hyperlink, the target URL appears. If you want it to display different text, follow steps **1** to **5** above, and then click the ScreenTip button. Type the desired text in the ScreenTip text box in the Set Hyperlink ScreenTip dialog box, and then click OK.

Try This!

The easiest way to insert the hyperlink into the Address field in the Insert Hyperlink dialog box is to start in the browser with the Web page loaded. Highlight and copy the address line displayed in your browser. In step **5** above, press Ctrl+V to paste the URL. Next, proceed with step **6**.

Add a link to an
E-MAIL ADDRESS

You can make it easy for customers or potential customers to reach you when you include hyperlinks to your e-mail address in presentations. Links to e-mail addresses look just like regular hyperlinks, with text that is underlined to differentiate it from regular text. When the presentation is in Slide Show Mode, the hyperlink is clickable.

When links to e-mail addresses are clicked, the viewer's default e-mail client is opened, a new e-mail message is created, and the message is preaddressed to the e-mail address specified. When

viewers finish with the e-mail message, they must intentionally return to PowerPoint to complete viewing the presentation, so you might want to include links to e-mail addresses at the end of your presentation so you do not risk losing viewers before they are finished with the presentation.

You can also specify the subject line for use by those sending a message. For example, to easily identify messages received from clicking the link, you can specify a subject line, such as Photo of the Month Entry.

① Highlight the text to which you want to insert a hyperlink.

② Click Insert.

③ Click Hyperlink.

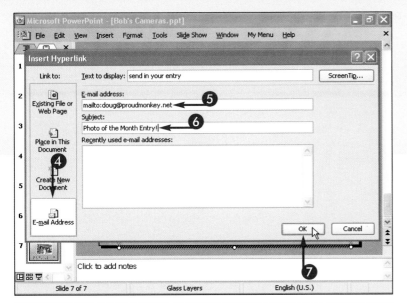

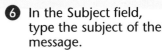

The Insert Hyperlink dialog box appears.

④ Click E-mail Address.

⑤ In the E-mail address field, type the complete e-mail address of the message's intended recipient.

⑥ In the Subject field, type the subject of the message.

⑦ Click OK.

The Insert Hyperlink dialog box closes.

⑧ Press F5 to preview the slide in Slide Show Mode.

The presentation opens in Slide Show Mode with the hyperlink inserted onto the slide.

Picture of the Month!

- Be sure to *send in your entry* for next month's Picture of the Month!

TIPS

Did You Know?

A hyperlink is also differentiated from normal text by its font color. If your presentation does not use a Design Template, hyperlinks are blue by default. If your presentation does use a Design Template, the Design Template determines the hyperlink font color.

Change It!

When you hover your mouse over a hyperlink to an e-mail address while in Slide Show Mode, it appears as "mailto:<alias> subject:<subject>," which is hardly a user-friendly ScreenTip. To change the ScreenTip to something friendlier, follow steps **1** to **5**, and then click the ScreenTip button. Type the new ScreenTip text in the ScreenTip text box in the Set Hyperlink ScreenTip dialog box, and then click OK.

Explain it better with
EQUATIONS

If presenting material that contains equations is part of your job, you know that creating and formatting equations can be cumbersome because they can include symbols, characters, and shapes that are not found on a standard keyboard and would take significant time to draw by hand. The Equation Editor is a program that comes with PowerPoint that eases the creation and editing of equations.

The Equation Editor is not included on any of the default toolbars or menus. You must add the Equation Editor to one of the toolbars so that you can easily access it in the future. After the Equation Editor button is visible on a toolbar, you can click it to open the Equation Editor.

The Equation Editor allows you to type formulas or parts of formulas from samples that look like the equation you seek to create and to easily insert equation-specific symbols and characters. You can choose from templates for fences, fractions, radicals, subscripts, superscripts, summations, integrals, underbars, overbars, and more.

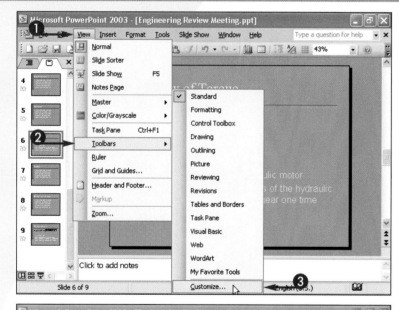

① Click View.

② Click Toolbars.

③ Click Customize.

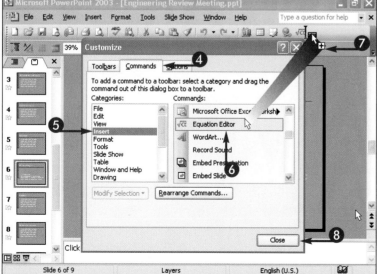

The Customize dialog box appears.

④ Click the Commands tab.

⑤ In the Categories section, click Insert.

⑥ In the Commands section, scroll down to Equation Editor.

⑦ Click and drag the Equation Editor onto one of the visible toolbars.

The Equation Editor button (√α̅) appears on the toolbar.

⑧ Click Close on the Customize dialog box.

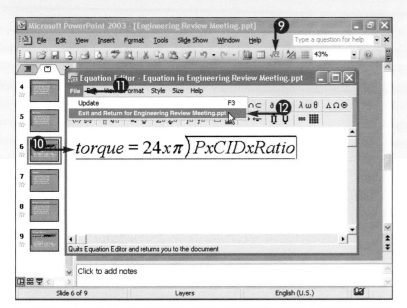

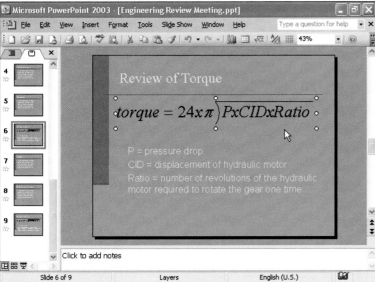

The Customize dialog box closes.

9 Click the Equation Editor button.

The Equation Editor dialog box appears.

10 Type your equation.

11 Click File.

12 Click Exit and Return.

The equation appears in your slide.

TIPS

Attention!
You may be prompted to install the Equation Editor after step **9** above. When prompted, click Yes to install it.

Did You Know?
You can edit an equation after it has been inserted into a slide. Simply double-click the equation; the Equation Editor opens with the equation ready for updating.

Caution!
The Equation Editor inserts equations as objects into slides. You cannot edit the font; it will always appear black. Therefore, if you place your equation on a slide with a black background, you will not be able to see it. Instead, you can create a rectangle with a light color and place the equation on top of it. You can freely resize the equation as desired.

Type specialized
CHARACTERS AND SYMBOLS

You can type characters that are not available on your keyboard when you insert symbols into your slides. You can use symbols for business purposes to type special characters like copyright (©), registered trademark (®), or trademark (™). You can also use characters from foreign alphabets or type emoticons, such as ☺ or ☻, to add feeling or emotion to slides.

You can also use symbols to create borders. For example, you can create a border by typing a specific symbol repeated across the top of a slide. You can

also highlight important text with symbols. For example, you can insert an arrow symbol before key items in a bulleted list.

Each font has its own collection of symbols. If you use a specific font in your presentation, you may need to use a different font for the symbol you want to use. For example, if you use an Arial font in your presentation, but you want to insert a check box symbol (☑), you will find it in the Wingdings font.

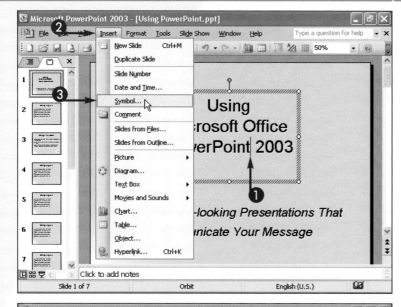

1 Click where you want to insert a symbol.

2 Click Insert.

3 Click Symbol.

The Symbol dialog box appears.

4 Click here and select the font you want to use.

5 Click the symbol you want to insert into your slide.

6 Click Insert.

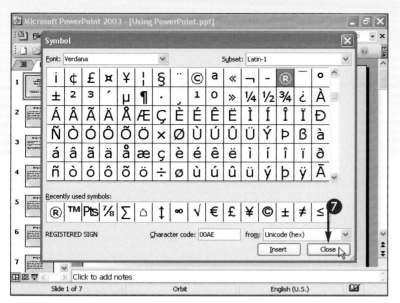

⑦ Click Close.

⑧ Repeat steps **1** to **7** for each symbol you want to insert into your slide.

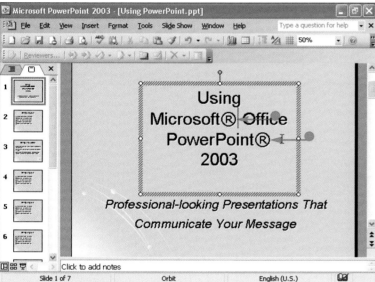

● The symbols appear in your slide.

TIPS

Caution!

When you insert a symbol, the Symbol dialog box remains open after the insertion. You can continue to insert symbols, but if you do, they will appear next to one another. If you do not want to have to reopen the Symbol dialog box each time you want to insert a symbol, you can insert all that you will need at one time and in one location, and then cut and paste them to the location desired.

Did You Know?

You can fully edit the formatting of symbols you have inserted into your slides. You can change font color, font size, and even add shadows, just as you would with any other text.

Add an Excel spreadsheet to
LEVERAGE DATA

You can save time and reduce the need to retype data when you insert an Excel spreadsheet into your slide. Reusing existing Excel spreadsheets reduces the risk of error that is introduced when you retype data. For example, instead of typing sales data into a presentation, you can insert data from an existing Excel spreadsheet directly into your slide.

When you insert an Excel spreadsheet into your presentation, the entire spreadsheet appears in its original format. When you click the object that

represents that file, the menu options change to give you Excel functionality from directly within PowerPoint. For example, you can select and delete columns, edit data, and use tools like AutoFormat.

Because most Excel spreadsheets are not designed for presentation on a large screen, you will most likely want to adjust font sizes to make the data easier to read. You can do this by highlighting the text and using the standard tools in PowerPoint to increase the font size.

❶ Click Insert.

❷ Click Object.

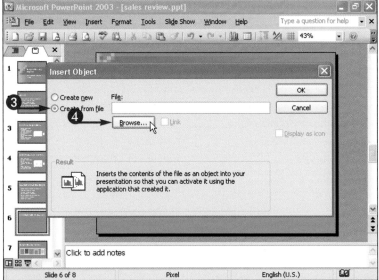

The Insert Object dialog box appears.

❸ Click the Create from file option (○ changes to ◉).

❹ Click Browse.

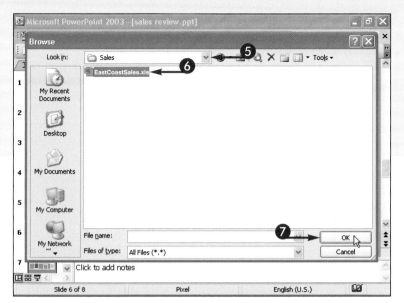

The Browse dialog box appears.

⑤ Click here and select the folder in which the spreadsheet is located.

⑥ Click the Excel spreadsheet you want to insert into the slide.

⑦ Click OK.

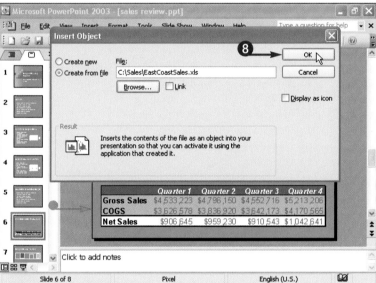

The Insert Object dialog box appears.

⑧ Click OK.

● The spreadsheet inserts into the slide.

TIPS

Did You Know?

You can resize the spreadsheet object by clicking and dragging the object borders.

Try This!

You can link the original spreadsheet so that if the spreadsheet changes, data on the slide automatically changes. To link them, follow steps **1** to **8** above, and then in the Insert Object dialog box, click the Link option (☐ changes to ☑).

Did You Know?

When you make changes to the content in the spreadsheet from within PowerPoint, it does not change the original spreadsheet. Therefore, you can delete columns that are not needed in a specific presentation without changing the original spreadsheet.

Add an Excel spreadsheet to
CALCULATE DATA

You can save time by inserting Excel spreadsheet tools directly into a slide. You can take advantage of the calculation, formatting, conditional formatting, and functional capabilities in Excel while you continue to do your work in PowerPoint.

If your slides routinely include information that requires calculations, you may be accustomed to using a calculator and then typing the results into a PowerPoint table. Instead, you can insert Excel spreadsheet capabilities directly into the slide so that the calculations take place where the data resides.

For example, in a slide for a flower shop that details a type of arrangement, you can calculate sales tax and create totals directly on your slide. When the price of the bouquet changes, you can edit the spreadsheet in the slide. The sales tax and totals automatically adjust for you.

When you are not editing the spreadsheet, it appears as an object on the slide, and the menus return to standard PowerPoint menus. When you click the spreadsheet object to edit it, menu options are updated to reflect editing options.

① Click Insert.

② Click Object.

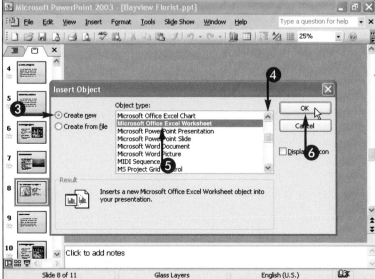

The Insert Object dialog box appears.

③ Click the Create new option (○ changes to ◉).

④ In the Object type section, scroll down to locate the type of object you want to insert into your presentation.

⑤ Click Microsoft Office Excel Worksheet.

⑥ Click OK.

An empty spreadsheet appears in the slide.

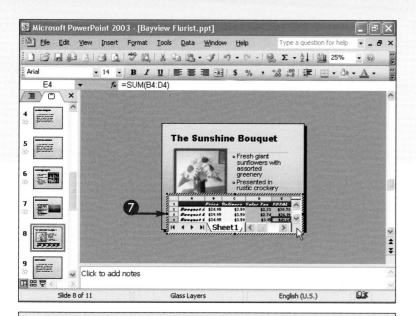

7 Type your data and use formatting tools as in Excel.

8 Press F5 to view the presentation in Slide Show Mode.

60

DIFFICULTY LEVEL

The presentation opens in Slide Show Mode with the Excel spreadsheet appearing as a table.

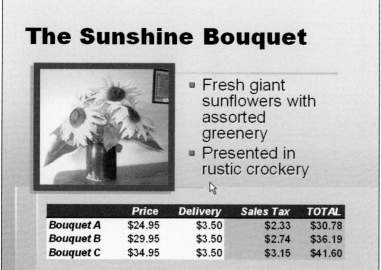

The Sunshine Bouquet

- Fresh giant sunflowers with assorted greenery
- Presented in rustic crockery

	Price	Delivery	Sales Tax	TOTAL
Bouquet A	$24.95	$3.50	$2.33	$30.78
Bouquet B	$29.95	$3.50	$2.74	$36.19
Bouquet C	$34.95	$3.50	$3.15	$41.60

TIPS

Try This!

Once your data is entered into the Spreadsheet Object, you can use AutoFormat to give it a professional look. Highlight the area to which you want to apply the AutoFormat, click Format, and then AutoFormat. Click the AutoFormat style you want to use, and then click OK.

More Options!

To resize the Spreadsheet Object, click it, and then click one of the small black squares (■) on the edge of the object. Click and drag until the edge is against the existing data. You may need to repeat this for each side you want to resize.

Did You Know?

When the Spreadsheet Object data appears on a slide, it looks like a table to the viewer.

Tell your story with
ILLUSTRATED CHARTS

You can use charts to illustrate important financial or numerical data. Charts help turn data into information, which makes it easier to identify trends and relationships. For example, you can greatly improve a table containing a list of financial results when you turn it into a chart that helps viewers identify variances or areas that need improvement.

PowerPoint charts use Microsoft Excel chart tools, but you do not need to know how to use Excel to be successful in using charts. When you insert a chart

into a slide, a sample chart is inserted with sample data opened in a datasheet for you to edit. You can type your data over the sample data, and as you do, the chart updates automatically. This allows you to create a chart to suit your needs without leaving PowerPoint or learning another tool.

The slide's Design Template determines the fonts that are used in the charts and the colors that are used on the bars to make your charts blend in with other elements in your slides.

① Click Insert.

② Click Chart.

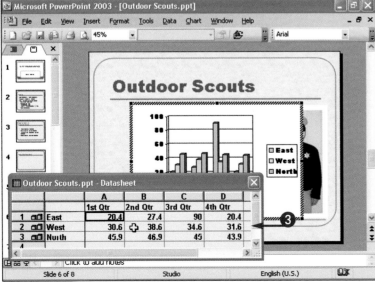

A sample chart and associated datasheet are inserted into the slide.

③ Click inside the datasheet.

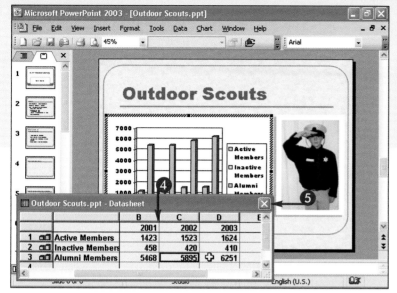

④ Type the data on which you want to base the chart.

The chart updates automatically with your new data.

⑤ Click ☒ to close the datasheet.

⑥ Click the slide outside the chart area to exit from chart editing.

⑦ Press F5 to view the presentation in Slide Show Mode.

The presentation opens in Slide Show Mode and the slide contains your custom chart.

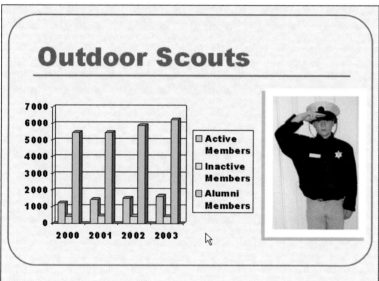

TIPS

Change It!

You can change the default chart to any of the other chart styles, including Bar, Line, Pie, and more. Right-click the chart, click Chart Type, and then click the chart style in the Chart type section. Click OK, and the chart is changed.

Try This!

You can edit charts after they have been inserted. Double-click the Chart Object to open the chart and the corresponding data sheet.

Did You Know?

You can edit the fonts used in charts by right-clicking the text you want to reformat, and then clicking the Format option. When the Format dialog box opens, click the Font tab and make the desired edits. Then click OK, and the font updates.

Make a point when you
CONNECT GRAPHICS

You can connect graphics to help illustrate timelines and relationships. Connectors are straight or curved lines or arrows that connect two or more drawing objects, such as AutoShapes, images, or other graphics. Connectors automatically anchor themselves to the midpoint of a side of an object, saving you time because you no longer have to painstakingly click and drag lines to try to meet exactly at an object's edge.

For example, in a diagram that contains six boxes that illustrate key concepts, you can demonstrate

relationships by drawing an arrow from one box to the next. When you use connectors, this is made easy because you simply click the connector you want to use, click near the right edge of the first box, near the left edge of the second box, and the connector is automatically anchored to the midpoints on each with perfectly straight lines connecting them. Even better, if you move one of the boxes, the lines stay connected, making editing diagrams easier than ever.

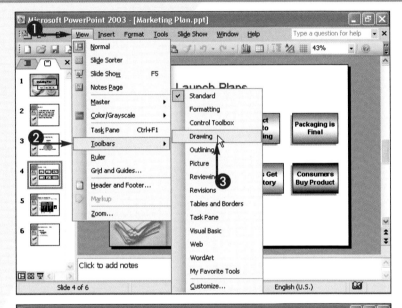

① Click View.

② Click Toolbars.

③ Click Drawing.

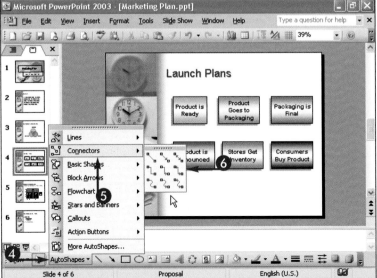

The Drawing toolbar appears.

④ Click AutoShapes.

⑤ Click Connectors.

⑥ Click the connector you want to use.

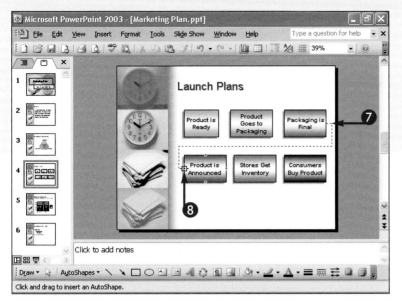

#62

When you hover over objects, a connection point displays on each side and corner, depending on the type of connector you select.

7 Click one of the connection points on the object from which you want to start the connector.

8 Click one of the connection points on the object to which you want to end the connector.

The connector appears between the shapes.

9 Repeat steps **4** to **8** for each connector desired.

The slide appears with the connectors.

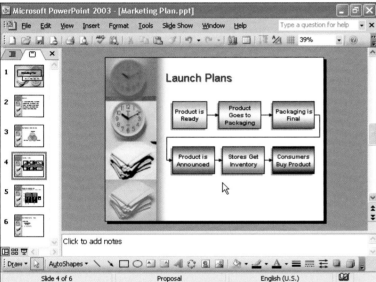

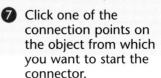

TIPS

Did You Know?

There are three types of connectors. Straight connectors use a straight line, Elbow connectors use straight lines and right angles, and Curved connectors use curved lines.

Change It!

You can easily move a connector from one object to another. Simply click the end of the connector you want to move, and drag it to another drawing object.

Change It!

If you rearrange drawing objects, and the connectors now connect objects in a path that could be shortened, you can use Reroute connectors to fix the problem. Right-click a connector you want to reroute, and click Reroute connectors. The connector changes to take the shortest route between the connected objects.

Show relationships with
ORGANIZATION CHARTS

You can show relationships between employees when you insert an organization chart into your slide. Organization charts are diagrams that use AutoShapes to represent team members, and connectors to illustrate the relationships between them.

Organization Chart saves time because it not only creates a sample organization chart for you, it makes it easy to add or remove Subordinates, Coworkers, or Assistants at the appropriate levels in the organization. It also resizes the chart automatically as the number of represented employees grows.

Changing the names on organization charts is easy because all you have to do is click the AutoShape and start typing.

You can also rearrange team members on the organization chart by clicking and dragging their AutoShapes to the desired location. Colors for AutoShapes and the text used on them are determined by the Design Template used on your slide. When you are not editing the organization chart, it appears on your slide as the Organization Chart Object so you can freely add and edit text and graphics around it.

❶ Click Insert.

❷ Click Diagram.

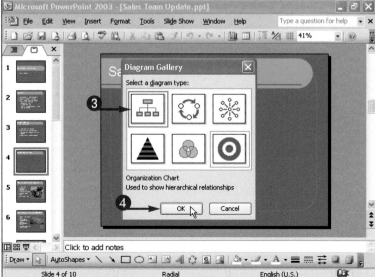

The Diagram Gallery dialog box appears.

❸ Click Organization Chart.

❹ Click OK.

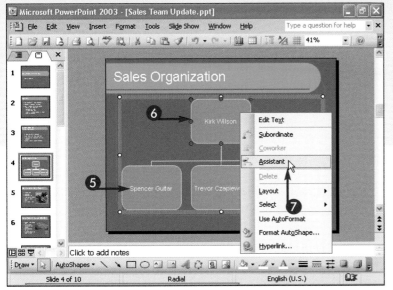

An organization chart is inserted into your slide.

⑤ Click one of the boxes and type a name.

⑥ Right-click a box.

The content menu appears.

⑦ Click the type of box you want to insert.

⑧ Repeat steps **5** to **7** to continue creating your organization chart.

⑨ Press F5 to view the slide in Slide Show Mode.

The presentation appears in Slide Show Mode with the organization chart in the slide.

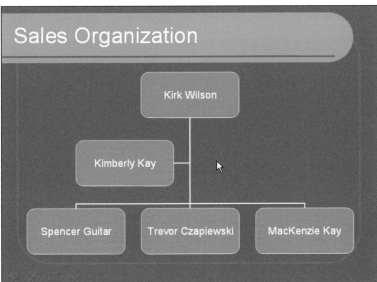

Change It!

You can change the style of the organization chart. Click the box representing the highest-level manager, right-click the organization chart, and then click Show Organization Chart Toolbar. Click the Layout ⌄, and then click the style you want to use.

Caution!

You cannot add a Coworker at the top level. The organization chart assumes that there is only one top-level manager.

Did You Know?

You can change the colors of the AutoShapes. Double-click the box you want to change, and in the Format AutoShape dialog box click the Colors and Lines tab. Click the Color ⌄, click the color you want to use, and then click OK.

Get your presentation noticed with
INK ANNOTATIONS

You can use your new Tablet PC with its pen input device to create Ink Annotations. Ink Annotations are like handwritten notes that lie on top of your slides. Ink Annotations can be used in Slide Show Mode or while you are editing slides. When you create Ink Annotations, they are saved with the presentation and are visible thereafter even by users who do not have or use Tablet PCs.

Ink Annotations can be particularly useful when you collaborate with a team on presentation content. You can add an Ink Annotation on a slide asking a team member to investigate or research a topic. You can even sketch out how you want a slide to appear when finished to help the team member responsible for the slide.

There are several pen styles from which to choose, including Ballpoint, Felt Tip, and Highlighters. Each pen style gives the Ink Annotations a different shape or width. You can also choose from a variety of Ink colors, with the default colors coming from the slide's Design Template.

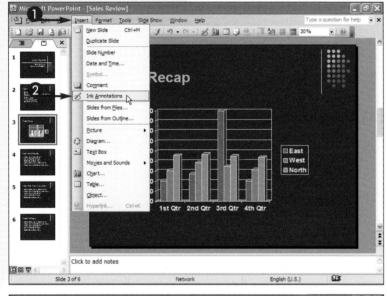

① Click Insert.

② Click Ink Annotations.

The Ink Annotations dialog box appears.

③ Click the Pen Style down arrow.

④ Click the pen style and color you want to use.

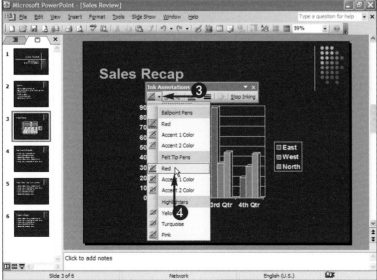

5 Click the Line Color.

6 Click the color you want to use.

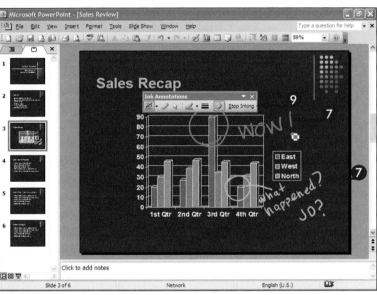

7 Ink the slide as desired.

8 Repeat steps **3** to **7** to continue inking in a different pen style or color.

9 Click Stop Inking when you are finished.

The Ink stays on the slide.

TIPS

Try This!
To use Ink Annotations during presentations, you must first place your Tablet PC input device pen over the lower part of the slide, tap the arrow on the Slide Show toolbar, and then tap the pen you want to use.

Customize It!
You can also use Ink colors that are not in the Design Template you are using. Follow steps **1** to **5** above, and click More Line Colors. In the Colors dialog box, click the color you want to use. Click OK.

Try This!
You can erase Ink Annotations. Click the Erase button (⬜) on the Ink Annotations toolbar, and then tap the Annotation you want to erase.

Expand Your Audience by Publishing to the Web

You can greatly expand your audience by publishing your presentations with Internet access. When you publish presentations to an intranet or Internet server, the presentations load as Web pages and are viewable even by those who do not have PowerPoint.

If you have access rights to a Web server, you can publish your presentation directly to the Internet, with no requirement for a separate Web publishing program. You can also use Web Page Preview to view how your presentation will look before you publish it to a Web site.

When a presentation is saved to the Web, the presentation's outline is used to create a list of hyperlinks to each slide to make it easy for

viewers to navigate to the slides in your presentation. You can specify the colors, the fonts, and even the page title that appears at the top of the page to make the Web presentation your own. You can also specify the alternative text that appears while an image is loading on a Web-based presentation.

If you know the screen resolution at which viewers will have their monitors set, you can create your presentation to look custom-made for that screen resolution. You can even optimize your presentation to work best on a specific brand or version of browser. Once your presentation is posted to the Web, you can easily link to it from text or graphics in another presentation.

Top 100

PREVIEW YOUR PRESENTATION
as a Web page

You can save time by using the Web Page Preview option to see how your presentation will look online. Long presentations that contain many graphics can take a few minutes to publish as a Web page. Web Page Preview allows you to see how your presentation is going to appear online without waiting for your computer to send the files to a Web server.

When you use Web Page Preview, PowerPoint creates an online presentation that displays in your browser.

It creates the presentation in the Single File Web Page file format, ending with an .mhtml extension. Single File Web Pages allow you to distribute a single file that plays a series of Web pages. This is important because Web-based presentations normally include many separate HTML files and a separate folder containing all of the graphics files. The Single File Web Page format allows you to see what viewers will see if you create and then give them a presentation in Single File Web Page format.

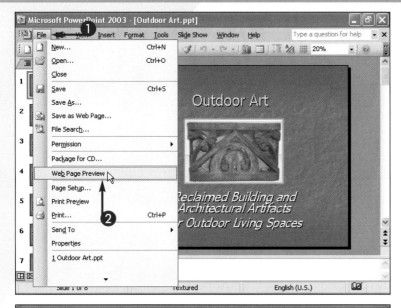

❶ Click File.

❷ Click Web Page Preview.

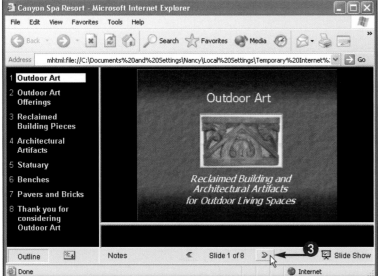

The presentation appears in the browser.

❸ Click the slide advancement right arrow to preview your presentation.

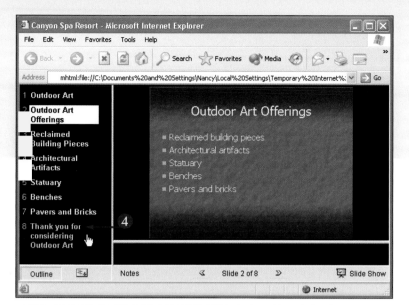

The presentation advances to the next slide.

④ Click one of the slides listed in the outline area to preview.

DIFFICULTY LEVEL

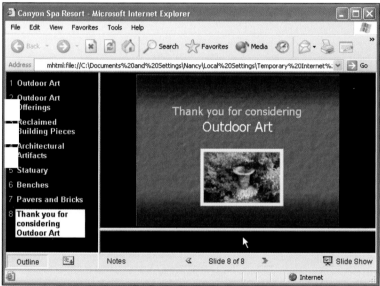

The presentation advances to the specific slide.

TIPS

Caution!

Web Page Preview creates a temporary file on your computer. If you want to create an online presentation to use, follow the steps in Task #66. Otherwise, the presentation is removed when you remove temporary files from your computer.

Did You Know?

By default, an online presentation displays the Outline, the Presentation, and the Notes panes. If you click Outline, the Outline pane is removed. If you click Notes, the Notes pane is removed.

Did You Know?

You can view the presentation in full screen by clicking the Slide Show link when the presentation is in Preview.

More Options!

After you have finished viewing the online presentation, close the browser by clicking ☒. PowerPoint appears with the presentation still loaded.

Turn your presentation into an
ONLINE RESOURCE

You can make your presentation widely available when you use the Save as Web Page option. By default, the Save as Web Page option creates a single file in the Single File Web Page format that allows users to double-click the file and then see a Web-based presentation that displays Outline, Notes, and Presentation panes. Viewers can easily navigate between all of the slides as well.

Once you have used the Save as Web Page option to create a Single File Web Page, you can post it on a

file server, an intranet, or Internet Web server for anyone to access and view. Users can double-click the file from an e-mail message or network location to open their browser and load the presentation. When users click a link to the presentation, they are prompted to open the presentation in their browser, or save it to their computer's hard drive. The ability to save the entire presentation to the hard drive makes Single File Web Pages an attractive way to distribute your presentations.

① Click File.

② Click Save as Web Page.

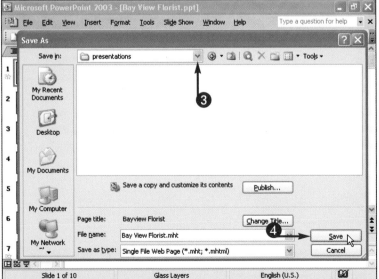

The Save As dialog box appears.

③ Click here and select the folder in which you want to save the online presentation.

④ Click Save.

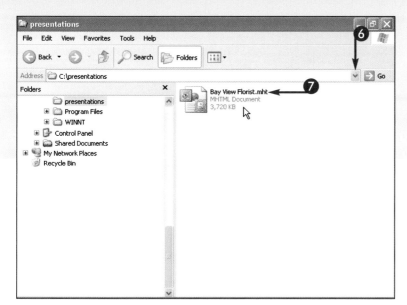

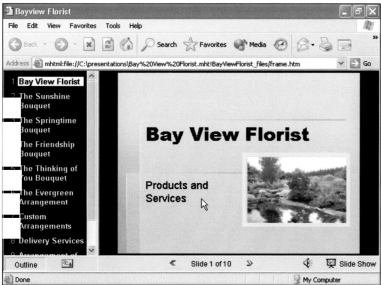

The presentation is saved for use in a Web browser.

⑤ Open Windows Explorer.

Note: *A fast way to open Windows Explorer is to click Start and Run, type* **explorer.exe***, and then press Enter.*

⑥ Click here and select the folder in which your browser-based presentation resides.

⑦ Double-click the file to open it.

The online presentation opens in the browser.

DIFFICULTY LEVEL

Did You Know?

You can create HTML pages instead of Single File Web Pages. The HTML option creates a single Web page for each slide. To save a presentation as HTML, follow steps **1** to **3** above, and then click the Save as type ⌄ and select Web Page. Proceed with step **4**. A folder is created that contains the HTML pages and a separate graphics folder.

Change It!

You can change the title that appears in the browser's title bar. After step **3**, click Change Title. In the Set Page Title dialog box, type the new page title in the Page title field. Click OK, and then proceed with step **4**.

PUBLISH YOUR PRESENTATION
directly to a Web site

You can make your presentation available to anyone with an Internet browser when you use Save as Web Page. Save as Web Page allows you to publish your online presentation directly to a Web server that supports the WebDAV standard, the FrontPage Server Extensions, SharePoint Team Services, or Windows SharePoint Services.

For example, instead of creating Single File Web Pages or HTML pages for your presentation and then using a Web site publishing or FTP program to transfer the files to your Web server, you can use Save as Web

Page. Save as Web Page allows you to specify a target server URL to which to publish, creates the necessary files, and then moves them to the Web server for you. Save as Web Page makes publishing to a Web server nearly as easy as saving a document.

Once the presentation has been published to the Web server, it can be linked to any other Web page. Viewers see the Outline, Notes, and Presentation panes, and can easily navigate between slides.

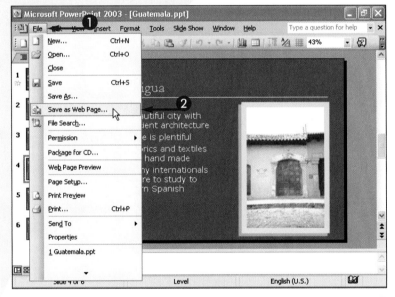

① Click File.

② Click Save as Web Page.

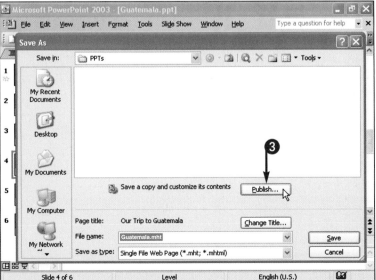

The Save As dialog box appears.

③ Click Publish.

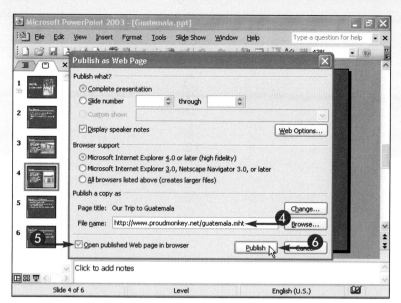

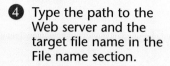

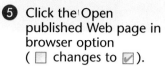

DIFFICULTY LEVEL

The Publish as Web Page dialog box appears.

④ Type the path to the Web server and the target file name in the File name section.

⑤ Click the Open published Web page in browser option (☐ changes to ☑).

⑥ Click Publish.

Note: You may receive a prompt to enter a user name and password in order to access the site.

The presentation is published to the Web server, and the browser opens with the presentation loaded.

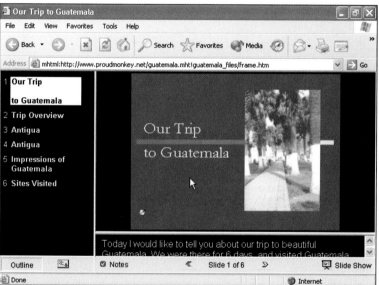

TIPS

Caution!

You must have the proper security and permissions to access the Web server. A prompt will ask you to supply a valid user name and password before you can access the Web server.

Important!

The path in step **4** is a combination of the Web site address and the file name. For example, if your Web site address is www.myserver.com, and the file name is myppt.mht, then the path you would type following http:// is **www.myserver.com/ myppt.mht**.

Did You Know?

You can save the presentation as an HTML page instead of a Single File Web Page. Follow steps **1** and **2**; in the Save As dialog box, click the Save as type ☑, and then click Web Page. Proceed with step **3**.

Specify the
DEFAULT FONTS
for Web-based presentations

You can control how your online presentation looks by changing the default fonts. Presentations often use fonts that are installed when PowerPoint is installed, but the same fonts may not be available on the systems viewers use to access a presentation online.

As part of the publishing process, you can specify default fonts used in Web presentations. You can specify proportional fonts and fixed-width fonts. Proportional fonts allow each character to take up a different amount of space. For example, a letter *i*

would be narrower than a letter *w* in a proportional font. Fixed-width fonts dedicate the same amount of space for every character.

You can specify proportional and fixed-width fonts. Most browsers specify the use of default proportional fonts (Web page fonts) and fixed-width fonts (Plain text fonts) when fonts are not specified on Web pages, or when the specified fonts are not available. By specifying the default fonts for a Web-based presentation, you can override your selected defaults.

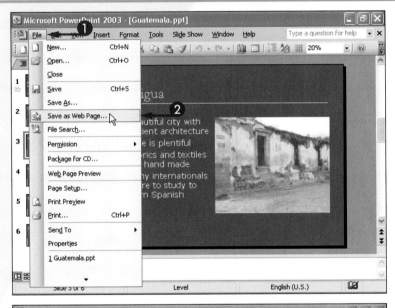

① Click File.

② Click Save as Web Page.

The Save As dialog box appears.

③ Click Publish.

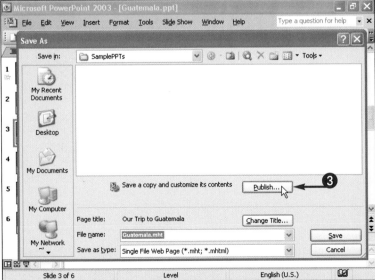

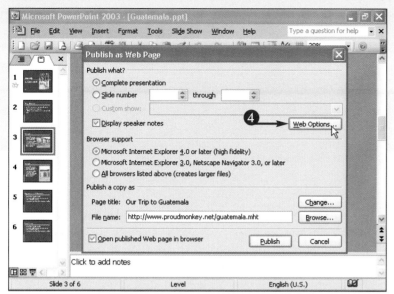

The Publish as Web Page dialog box appears.

④ Click Web Options.

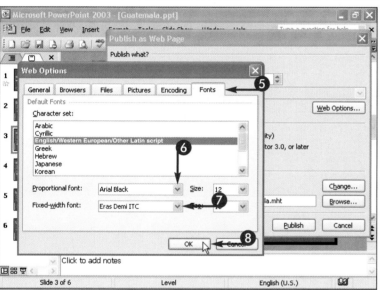

The Web Options dialog box appears.

⑤ Click the Fonts tab.

⑥ Click here and select the proportional font you want to use.

⑦ Click here and select the fixed-width font you want to use.

⑧ Click OK.

The Web Options dialog box closes.

⑨ To continue publishing, follow steps **3** to **6** in Task #67.

The presentation is published using the fonts you specified.

TIPS

Did You Know?
You can specify the default proportional font size. Follow steps **1** to **6** above, and then click the Size ⋁ to select the default proportional font size.

Did You Know!
You can specify the default fixed-width font size. Follow steps **1** to **7** above, and then click the Size ⋁ to select the default fixed-width font size.

Go International!
You can specify the default character set when you create presentations for an international audience. Follow steps **1** to **5** above. In the Character set section, scroll up or down to locate the character set you want to use, and then click to select it. Proceed with step **6**.

CUSTOMIZE COLORS
in Web-based presentations

You can customize the colors used in Web-based presentations to suit your tastes. By default, the Outline and Notes panes in online presentations have a black background with white fonts. Similarly, the area behind the slide is black. However, you can publish your presentations using colors that coordinate with your presentation's look and feel instead of using the default black.

You can change Web presentation colors during the publishing process. When you choose to use the Presentation colors (font color) option, PowerPoint uses the default colors and primary font color from the design template that is applied to your presentation. For example, if you use the Glass Layers Design Template in green, you may want the Outline, Notes, and Presentation panes to use the same green background as well.

Once preferences have been changed to match the presentation's colors, when the presentation is published to a Web format, the presentation blends in with the Outline, Notes, and Presentation panes. Coordination of the background colors makes for a more polished and professional-looking online presentation.

1 Click File.

2 Click Save as Web Page.

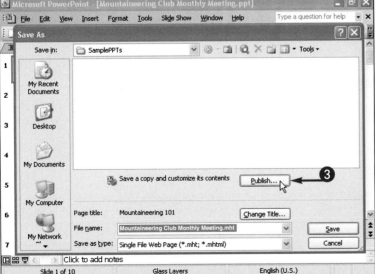

The Save As dialog box appears.

3 Click Publish.

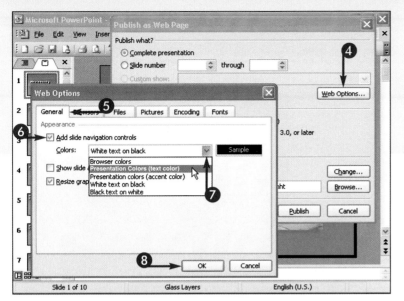

The Publish as Web Page dialog box appears.

④ Click Web Options.

The Web Options dialog box appears.

⑤ Click the General tab.

⑥ Click the Add slide navigation controls option (☐ changes to ☑).

⑦ Click here and select the color option you want to use.

⑧ Click OK.

⑨ To continue publishing, follow steps **3** to **6** in Task #67.

The presentation is published with Web interface using your color selections.

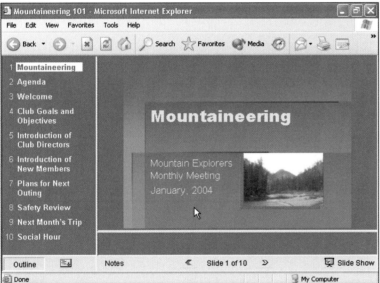

TIPS

Caution!

You can change the default background color to the default background color of the viewer's browser. Simply follow the steps above, but in step **7** click Browser colors instead of Presentation colors (text color). However, results will be unpredictable.

Did You Know?

You can change the default black background with white text to white background with black text. Follow the steps above, but in step **7** click Black text on white instead of Presentation colors (text color).

Did You Know?

You can use the Design Template's accent font color instead of using the Design Template's primary font color. Follow the steps above, but in step **7** click Presentation colors (accent color) instead of Presentation colors (text color).

CHANGE THE TITLE
for a Web-based presentation

You can change text that appears at the top of a viewer's Web browser when you create online presentations by changing the title bar text. The title bar appears at the top left of the browser window, and helps users identify the page that they are viewing.

Page titles should be descriptive enough to give viewers context for what page they are on, but not so long that that they take effort to read. Most Web site visitors glance quickly at page titles to make

sure that they are on the right page, but do not spend time studying them.

Page titles can draw attention to important messages. For example, if your presentation is promoting a new product or service, you can include special characters, such as *!*, ***, or *#*, in the page title to draw attention to it or include information about the sale in the page title. Because this information appears in the user's browser, it is another good way to communicate a message to viewers of your online presentation.

1 Click File.

2 Click Save as Web Page.

The Save As dialog box appears.

3 Click Change Title.

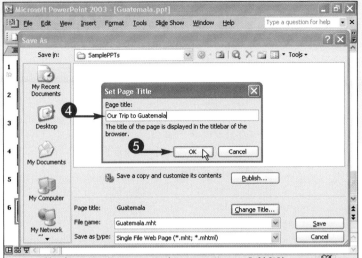

The Set Page Title dialog box appears.

④ Type the page title in the Page title field.

⑤ Click OK.

The Set Page Title dialog box closes.

⑥ To continue publishing, follow steps **3** to **6** in Task #67.

 # 70

DIFFICULTY LEVEL

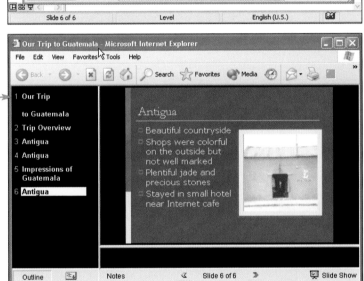

● The presentation is published with the specified title on the browser title bar.

TIPS

Did You Know?

Page titles are also used when viewers switch from program to program by pressing Alt+Tab. Text length is limited in the program switching dialog box, so you should make sure that page titles are not too long.

Try This!

If you have multiple browser windows open and then click the Windows Task Bar to see what browser window you want to switch to, the page title appears. This space is limited, so be sure to limit page title length.

Did You Know?

Because some Internet search engines use page titles to help users search for Web content, use page titles that utilize key words by which users may search.

Make images accessible when you set
ALTERNATIVE TEXT

You can make images more meaningful in online presentations for users on slow Internet connections or with visual impairments by setting alternative text for images. Alternative text on images instructs browsers to display text while images are loading or when images cannot be displayed.

Users with slow Internet connections often set their browsers to not display images by default. That allows them to quickly bring up Web pages because images are often the biggest elements to download on pages. If you do not specify text that should

appear in place of images, the user sees only an icon that explains that an image is missing. If you specify alternative text for images, the viewer sees the specified text in place of the image.

Setting alternative text is useful for visitors with impaired vision who use reader programs to read Web pages for them. When an image has alternative text set, the reader program will read the alternative text, which adds to the value of the presentation and makes your work more accessible.

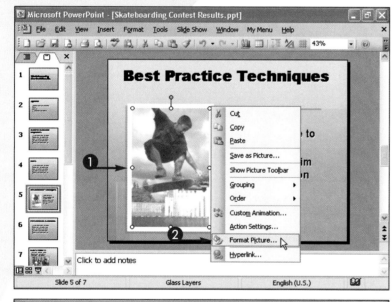

1 Right-click the picture to which you want to assign alternative text.

The content menu appears.

2 Click Format Picture.

The Format Picture dialog box appears.

3 Click the Web tab.

4 In the Alternative text box, type the alternative text.

5 Click OK to close the dialog box.

The alternative text is assigned to the image.

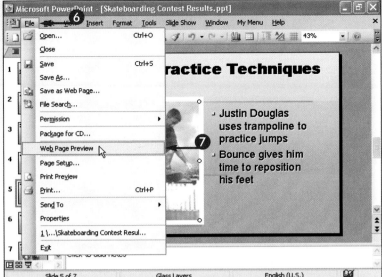

6 Click File.

7 Click Web Page Preview.

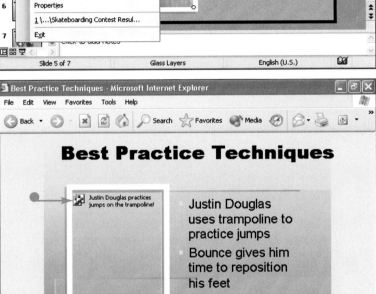

● The alternative text displays while the image loads.

TIPS

Caution!
Alternative text can be as long as you want, but not all browsers will display all of the text. Therefore, it is a good idea to keep alternative text relatively brief.

Try This!
You can add alternative text to drawing objects and AutoShapes. In step **1** above, replace the picture with a drawing object or an AutoShape.

Try This!
You can see how alternative text will appear in the browser by using Web Page Preview. Click File and then Web Page Preview.

Did You Know?
Some Internet search engines use the words in alternative text as key words by which users can search. This is another good reason to assign alternative text to every image or AutoShape and to use words that users may search on the Internet.

Change the target
SCREEN RESOLUTION
for Web-based presentations

You can optimize your presentation for a specific screen resolution to give it the best possible appearance. When you publish your presentation online, it is often difficult to anticipate the size at which viewers will have their screens set. One user may have an older monitor that is set at a smaller size of 640 pixels wide by 480 pixels high. Another may have a newer, larger monitor that is set at 1024 x 768.

However, today's corporate users are likely to have similar hardware and screen resolutions. When you

know that users have newer monitors, for example, you can predict that most will view presentations at 800 x 600 or 1024 x 768. Therefore, you can set PowerPoint to publish online presentations in a format that looks best at those screen resolutions.

You can also set the screen resolution to work best on smaller screens, such as those used on notebook or handheld devices. For example, a presentation for a sales force using handheld devices could be optimized for 544 x 376.

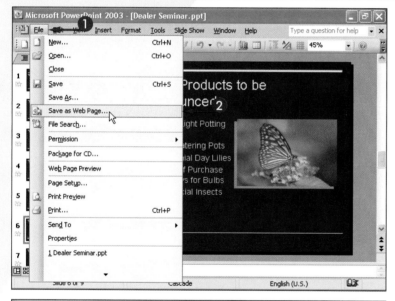

① Click File.

② Click Save as Web Page.

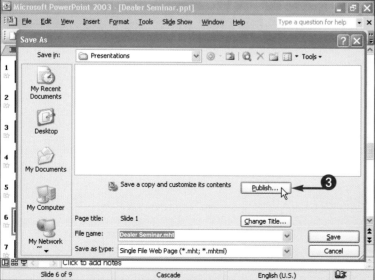

The Save As dialog box appears.

③ Click Publish.

DIFFICULTY LEVEL

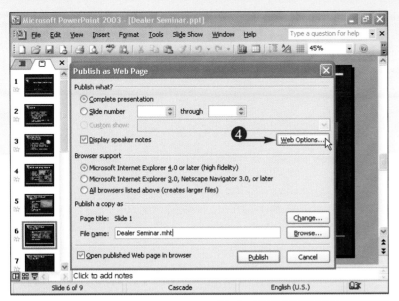

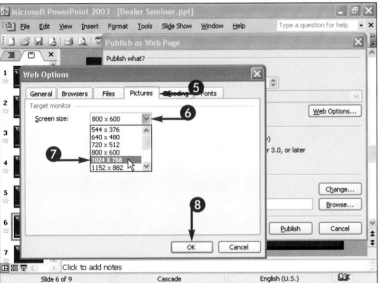

The Publish as Web Page dialog box appears.

④ Click Web Options.

The Web Options dialog box appears.

⑤ Click the Pictures tab.

⑥ Click the Screen size ⊡.

⑦ Click the desired screen size.

⑧ Click OK.

The target screen size is set, and the presentation is published optimized at the specified screen resolution.

⑨ To continue publishing, follow steps **3** to **6** in Task #67.

TIPS

Include It!

You can optimize the screen resolution when you want to display the content of a frame in another browser window. For example, if you publish at a smaller screen resolution, you can bring the presentation into another Web page and still have room for additional content.

Did You Know?

You can publish your presentation to display the slides with no Outline or Notes panes. In Task #69, after step **3** in the Publish as Web Page dialog box, click the Display speaker notes option (☑ changes to ☐), and in step **6** click the Add slide navigation controls option (☑ changes to ☐). Then proceed with step **8**.

OPTIMIZE YOUR PRESENTATION
for a specific browser

You can help assure that your online presentation is accessible by users with the most popular browsers when you optimize your presentation for specific browsers. You can accomplish this by selecting browser brands and versions with which you want to make sure that your presentation works well.

Options include Microsoft Internet Explorer 3.0 or later and Netscape Navigator 3.0 or later. Default Web presentations are optimized for Microsoft Internet Explorer 4.0 or later because the majority of Internet browsers used fall in this category. However,

if you are creating a presentation for use within your company and your company is standardized on Microsoft Office 2003 programs like PowerPoint 2003, you can instead choose to create presentations for Internet Explorer 6.0 or later because Office 2003 includes it. Conversely, if you are creating a Web presentation for use on the Internet, you may want to optimize your presentation for Internet Explorer 3.0 and Netscape Navigator 3.0 or later to make your presentation viewable by a broad array of users with a variety of Web browsers.

① Click File.

② Click Save as Web Page.

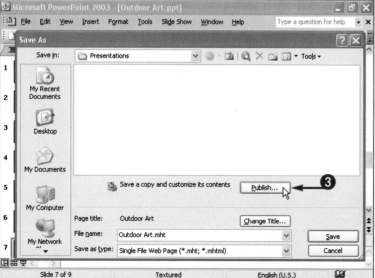

The Save As dialog box appears.

③ Click Publish.

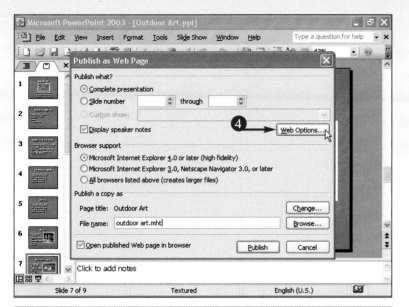

The Publish as Web Page dialog box appears.

④ Click Web Options.

The Web Options dialog box appears.

⑤ Click the Browsers tab.

⑥ Click the People who view this Web page will be using ⮟.

⑦ Click the browser or browser combination you want to target.

⑧ Click OK.

The presentation is published optimized for the chosen browser or browser combination.

⑨ To continue publishing, follow steps **3** to **6** in Task #67.

TIPS

Caution!

Online presentation files get larger as more browser brands and versions are supported because additional code is necessary to support features in older browsers. Be conservative in the range of browsers for which you choose to optimize your presentation. Optimizing your presentation for Internet Explorer 6.0 will create the smallest presentation and be the fastest to load. Conversely, presentations optimized for Internet Explorer 3.0 and Netscape Navigator 3.0 or later will create larger files and will load more slowly.

Caution!

Not all features in your presentation will work on all browser brands and versions. For example, some slide transitions and animations will not work on older browser versions.

LINK YOUR PRESENTATION
to another Web page

You can leverage your presentation by publishing it to a Web server and then linking to it from another presentation. For example, if you publish a presentation about your products to the Internet, you could link to it from a presentation about your company's marketing efforts.

The key to successfully linking to an online presentation is browsing to it, and then creating the hyperlink to it. When you publish an online presentation as a Single File Web Page, you are publishing to a path such as www.server.com/filename.mht, but when it is

viewed in the browser, it resolves to an address of mhtml:http://www.server.com/filename.mht!filename_files/frame.htm. You can link to the resolved address to make the presentation load as quickly as possible.

When you create a hyperlink to an online presentation, you can browse to the presentation to which you want to link. Once you browse to the page to which you want to link, you are returned to the presentation to complete the steps for creating the hyperlink.

① Highlight the text to which you want to apply a hyperlink.

② Click Insert.

③ Click Hyperlink.

The Insert Hyperlink dialog box appears.

④ Click the Browse the Web button.

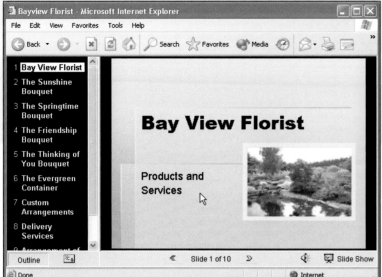

The browser opens.

5 Browse to the presentation to which you want to link.

6 Press Alt+Tab to return to PowerPoint.

#74

DIFFICULTY LEVEL

The Edit Hyperlink dialog box appears.

7 Click OK.

● The hyperlink to your presentation is added to the text.

TIPS

Try This!

You can create a hyperlink from a picture or an AutoShape. In step **1** above, click the picture or AutoShape instead of highlighting text, and then proceed with step **2**.

Try This!

You can create a hyperlink to a presentation that is located on a file share. Follow steps **1** to **3** above, and then click the Browse for File button (⊠) instead of the Browse the Web button (🔍).

Try This!

You can specify text to appear when you hover your mouse pointer over a hyperlink. Simply follow steps **1** to **3** above, and then click ScreenTip. In the Set Hyperlink ScreenTip dialog box, type the ScreenTip text. Click OK, and then proceed with step **4** above.

Collaborate with Others

You can enlist the help of others in reviewing or editing your presentations when you use collaboration features. You can safeguard your presentation by requiring a password in order to view it. You can also use new Information Rights Management to not only control access to a presentation, but control how the presentation can be used by those you do authorize to open it.

You can send presentations to others in e-mail messages to review, and when they are finished editing the presentations, they can easily return them to you. Reviewers' edits are easy to identify and then act upon, and you can even consolidate multiple versions of your presentation and see who made each change to it. You can also use comments to add notes to presentations without changing the content itself.

You can now send presentations to others for review as shared attachments. Shared attachments are stored on a central Web server running Windows SharePoint Services as a shared workspace. When users receive your presentation in an e-mail message, they are prompted to check to see if there is a more current version on the shared workspace, which assures that each user is working with the latest version of your presentation.

You can access and modify resources on your shared workspace from within PowerPoint. You can use your shared workspace to view document version information. You can even sign up to receive an e-mail message when anything on your shared workspace changes.

Top 100

Safeguard your presentation with a
PASSWORD

You can keep your presentation from being opened by unauthorized users when you assign a password to it. Passwords are a combination of characters that the user must type correctly before performing an action.

You can require one password for opening a presentation and another for editing a presentation. For example, if your presentation includes confidential sales information, you could require a password in order to open it. Similarly, if you have a presentation you want certain users to be able make

changes to and then save, you can create another password for the right to make changes to the presentation and then save them.

When users open a presentation that you have open- and edit- password protected, they are prompted for the password to open the presentation and then for a password to edit the presentation. If they do not have the edit password, they can open the presentation in read-only mode, which allows them to see the presentation but not make changes to it.

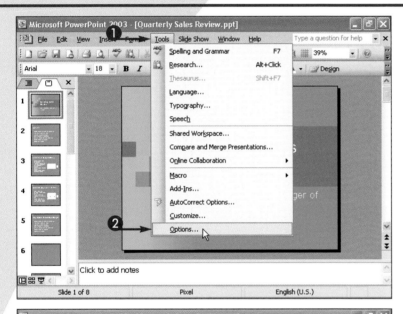

1 Click Tools.

2 Click Options.

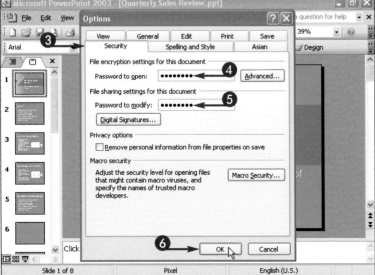

The Options dialog box appears.

3 Click the Security tab.

4 In the Password to open field, type the password for opening presentations.

5 In the Password to modify field, type the password for modifying presentations.

6 Click OK.

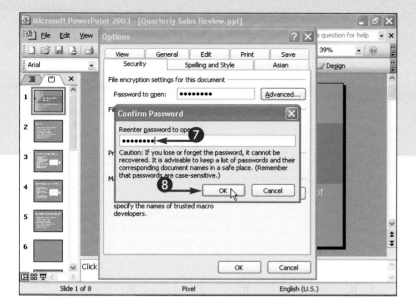

The Confirm Password dialog box appears.

75

⑦ In the Reenter password to open field, retype the password for opening presentations.

⑧ Click OK to confirm the password for opening the presentation.

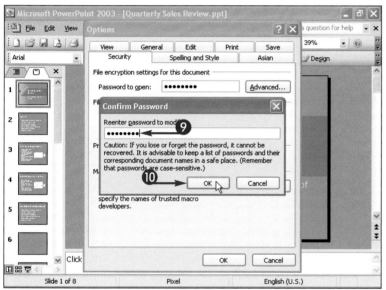

The Confirm Password dialog box appears.

⑨ In the Reenter password to modify field, retype the password for modifying presentations.

⑩ Click OK to confirm the password for editing the presentation.

The Confirm Password and Options dialog boxes close. The passwords for opening and modifying the presentation are set for the presentation.

TIPS

Caution!
Users can share passwords with others. For example, if you send the presentation attached to an e-mail message and include the password in the message body, the user can easily forward the message to someone else.

Important!
If you are going to require passwords for accessing your presentations, you should use strong passwords. Strong passwords use combinations of lower- and uppercase letters, numbers, and special symbols to make it more difficult for people to guess the password. For example, 4Apple$ is considered a strong password, while 4apples is not.

Caution!
Even if a user has only the password required to open a presentation, the user can use Save As to save it to another file.

Control presentation use with
INFORMATION RIGHTS MANAGEMENT

You can protect your presentation against unauthorized access, and even control how it is used once it is opened, with new Information Rights Management (IRM). IRM uses the Windows Rights Management service in Windows Server 2003 that helps companies set policies for how users can access and distribute company resources. For example, your company can determine that all presentations flagged as "company confidential" cannot be printed, forwarded, or saved as another filename.

If your company has not yet deployed Windows Server 2003 and IRM, you can still use it by

subscribing to the Microsoft Office Online Service. You can access IRM features by clicking File, and then Permission. When prompted, set up IRM capabilities by using Microsoft Passport to access the Office Online Service or by using your company's Microsoft Windows Accounts to manage the service.

Information Rights Management is different from simply assigning a password to a document. Instead, it allows only designated users with the appropriate credentials who are logged either into Passport or into your company's network to access the presentation.

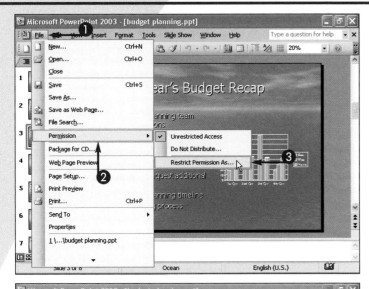

① Click File.

② Click Permission.

③ Click Restrict Permission As.

The Select User dialog box opens.

④ Click the user account you want to use.

⑤ Click OK.

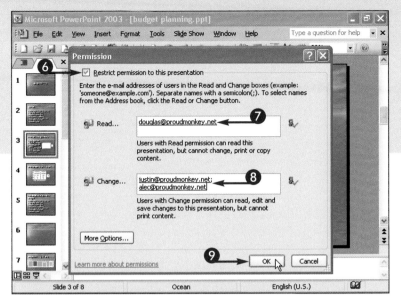

The Permission dialog box appears.

6 Click the Restrict permission to this presentation option (☐ changes to ☑).

7 In the Read section, type the e-mail addresses of people who have read access to this presentation.

8 In the Change section, type the e-mail addresses of people with permission to change this presentation.

9 Click OK.

The restricted access rights are set and listed in the Shared Workspace Task Pane.

#76

DIFFICULTY LEVEL

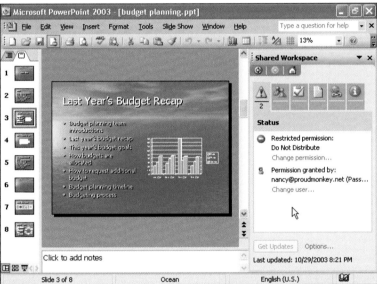

TIPS

Did You Know?

To use IRM, you must first access the IRM service. This is done by specifying your Microsoft Passport e-mail address when you use Office Online. You can specify your Windows account name, such as DOMAIN/alias, when you use your company's service.

Edition Alert!

To create IRM-protected presentations, you must have Microsoft Office Professional Edition 2003. If you have a version of PowerPoint 2003 that comes with another edition of Microsoft Office 2003, you can only read and, if permitted, edit IRM-protected presentations.

Attention!

Those who want to access the IRM-protected presentation must have either PowerPoint 2003 or an IRM add-on for Internet Explorer that is available free from the Microsoft Office Online Web site.

Enlist the help of others with
SEND FOR REVIEW

You can get others on your team to contribute to your presentation when you send it to them for review. Send for Review allows you to send your presentation to others via e-mail message attachments. When you use Send for Review, your e-mail client is automatically opened with a new message prepared with the presentation attached. Once you have addressed the message and included message content, you send the message just like any other e-mail message that contains an attachment.

When the presentation is sent for review in an e-mail message, change tracking is automatically enabled so that all changes the recipient makes to the presentation are flagged. When you open a presentation that has been edited by another person and change tracking has been enabled because the presentation was sent for review, you are asked if you want to merge the changes into your existing presentation. When you do so, the presentation opens with the Revisions Task Pane showing. The Revisions Task Pane is where you can see what changes were made to each slide and by whom.

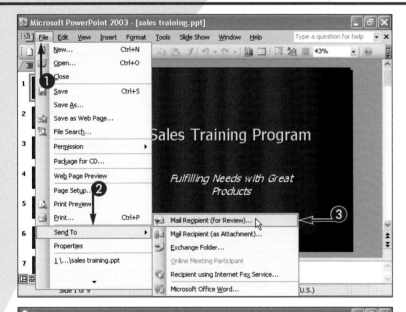

SEND PRESENTATION FOR REVIEW

1. Click File.
2. Click Send To.
3. Click Mail Recipient (for Review).

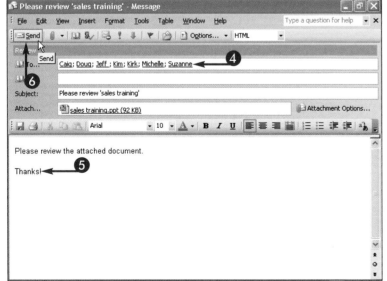

Your e-mail client opens with a new message with the presentation attached.

4. Type the e-mail addresses of the people you want to send the presentation to for review.

5. Type any desired text in the body of the e-mail message.

6. Click Send.

An e-mail message is sent to each recipient with the presentation attached and revisions turned on.

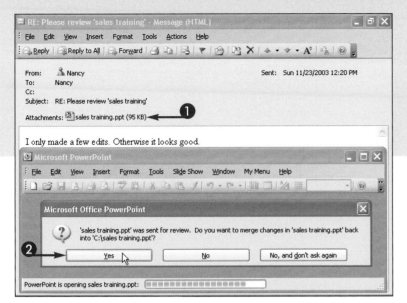

OPEN REVIEWED PRESENTATION

① Double-click the presentation you want to open.

Note: *You can also open the presentation in a network location by double-clicking it in Windows Explorer.*

The Microsoft Office PowerPoint dialog box appears.

② Click Yes when asked if you want to merge changes back into the presentation.

The presentation opens in PowerPoint and the Reviewing toolbar and the Revisions Task Pane appear.

Did You Know?

When you use Send for Review, the Please review the attached document text is automatically inserted into the message. Because you will likely be sending a presentation, not a document, you might want to change that text to better suit your message.

Return to Sender!

When you are the recipient of a presentation that was sent for review, you can send it back to the originator by clicking File, Send To, and then Original Sender. The presentation is returned to the originator with your revisions marked.

Attention!

When you make changes to a presentation sent to you for review, you are changing only your copy of the presentation. The original presentation is unchanged.

USE TRACK CHANGES
to identify revisions

When you work with others who are reviewing or editing your presentation, you can identify the changes that they made and then decide which ones you want to keep and which ones you want to disregard. For example, you could post your presentation to a network share, and then ask team members to make edits to it. You could also send your presentation to team members for review.

When you open a presentation that has been edited by others, you are asked whether you want to merge changes with your original presentation. When you

do so, the presentation opens with the Revisions Task Pane and the Reviewing toolbar visible. The Reviewing toolbar helps you quickly find the next change made in the presentation; the Revisions Task Pane helps you find out who made the change and exactly what was changed.

When multiple changes have been made on a slide, you can choose which changes you want to apply. This is important when you receive contradictory or conflicting comments from reviewers.

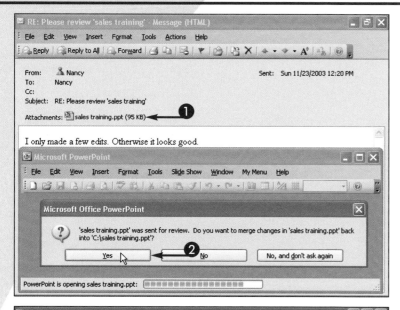

① Double-click the presentation you want to open.

Note: *You can also open the presentation from a network location by double-clicking it in Windows Explorer.*

The Microsoft Office PowerPoint dialog box appears.

② Click Yes when asked if you want to merge changes back into the presentation.

The presentation opens in PowerPoint, and the Reviewing toolbar and the Revisions Task Pane appear.

③ On the Reviewing toolbar, click the Next Item button.

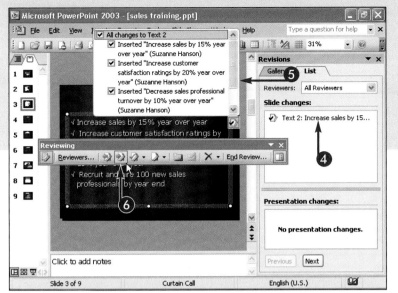

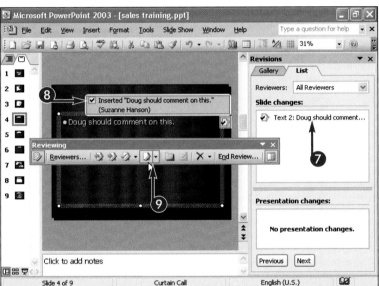

The Slide changes section in the Revisions Task Pane lists the revisions made on the slide.

78

④ Click the revision you want to review.

The revisions details list appears.

⑤ Click the option for the revisions you want to accept (☐ changes to ☑).

The selected revisions are made in the slide.

⑥ On the Reviewing toolbar, click the Next Item button.

The next revision appears in the Revisions Task Pane.

⑦ Click the revision you want to review.

⑧ Click the option for the revision you want to reject (☐ changes to ☑).

⑨ On the Reviewing toolbar, click the Unapply button.

The revision is removed from the slide.

⑩ Repeat steps **3** to **9** until all revisions have been addressed.

TIPS

Did You Know?

When you reject, or Unapply, a revision, you are choosing not to include it in a presentation. When you accept a revision, you are choosing to use it in the presentation.

Network It!

When you post a presentation to a network share, reviewers are prompted to save the presentation with revisions marked. If they do, only you, the author, can see everyone's revisions. The individuals who edited the presentation see only their revisions.

Caution!

While reviewing changes made to your presentation, if you choose to accept comments in a presentation, they will be visible to others who use the final presentation. However, comments are not visible in Slide Show Mode.

Use comments to
ADD NOTES

You can use Comments as a way to communicate with reviewers or insert a reminder into a slide. Comments are like electronic sticky notes that you can use to type any text you want.

Comments can be a great way to communicate with a presentation's author without changing the presentation itself. For example, if you want to remind the presentation's author to insert a new slide or do some additional research, changing the presentation content might not be an appropriate way to do it. Instead, you can insert a comment as a highly visible way to get the author's attention.

Comments inserted into a slide are displayed with a different color for each reviewer. They also display the name of the reviewer who made the comment and the date the comment was inserted or edited. When the comments are not opened, a small colored box is displayed that shows the initials of the person who inserted the comment plus a number. This allows one person to insert more than one comment on a page, such as NAB1, NAB2, and NAB3.

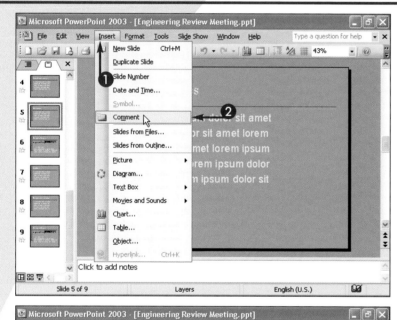

INSERT A NEW COMMENT

① Click Insert.

② Click Comment.

A blank comment is inserted into the slide.

③ Click the comment form, and then type your comments.

④ Click off the comment on the slide.

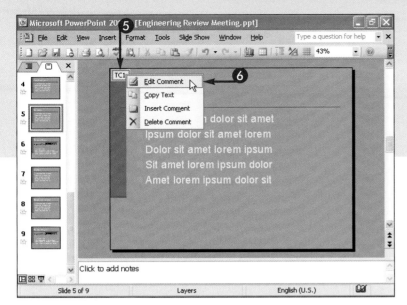

The comment form closes but the comment symbol remains.

5 Right-click the comment symbol.

The content menu appears.

6 Click Edit Comment.

#79

DIFFICULTY LEVEL

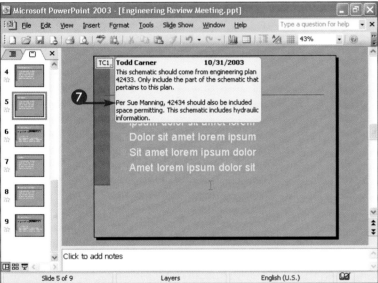

The comment form appears.

7 Click and then type to edit the comment.

TIPS

Name It!
You can change the name and initials that are displayed in Comments. Click Tools, and then Options. In the Options dialog box, click the General tab, change the name in the Name field, and then the initials in the Initials field. Click OK. Future Comments will use the new name and initials.

Caution!
If another reviewer edits your Comment, it will show that reviewer's name and initials, not yours. Similarly, if you edit another person's Comment, it will look like your Comment. Therefore, consider editing your own Comments, but add new Comments instead of editing the Comments of others.

Move It!
You can move a Comment on a slide by clicking and dragging it to a new location.

CONSOLIDATE FEEDBACK
from others

When you work with a team, it makes sense to collect feedback from team members. However, the process of reviewing presentations and the changes made by each team member can become cumbersome when you receive separate presentations from each team member. You can save time and make the process easier by combining all revised presentations when you use Compare and Merge Presentations.

When multiple presentations are merged into one, the Reviewing toolbar and the Revisions Task Pane appear. The Reviewing toolbar makes it easy to find each revision, and the Revisions Task Pane allows you to see a list of the changes and who made them. The Revisions Task Pane also allows you to see a list of changes made to the presentation overall, such as insertion of a new slide. You can click a change in the Revisions Task Pane and then see its effects on the slide. You can even use the Reviewing toolbar to choose to accept all changes made to a slide or to the entire presentation.

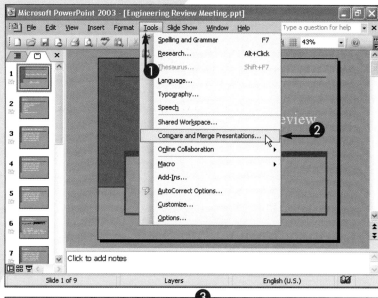

❶ Click Tools.

❷ Click Compare and Merge Presentations.

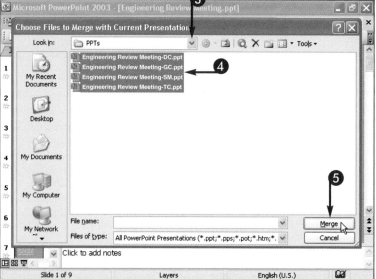

The Choose Files to Merge with Current Presentation dialog box appears.

❸ Click here and select the folder in which the presentations you want to merge with this presentation are located.

❹ Press Ctrl+click to select all of the files you want to merge with this presentation.

❺ Click Merge.

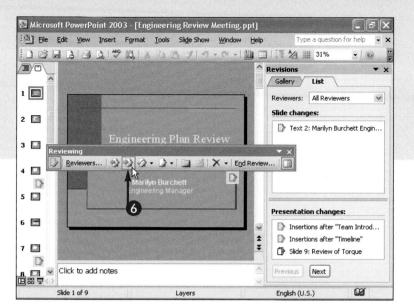

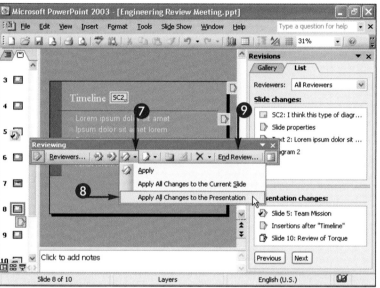

The presentations are merged, and the Revisions Task Pane and the Reviewing toolbar appear.

⑥ On the Reviewing toolbar, click the Next Item button to review changes.

 # 80

DIFFICULTY LEVEL

⑦ Click the Apply ⬝ on the Reviewing toolbar.

⑧ Click Apply All Changes to the Presentation.

All changes are made to the presentations.

⑨ Click End Review.

The Reviewing toolbar closes and the review cycle is finished.

Did You Know?

Compare and Merge Presentations compares presentations against the presentation that is currently open. Start by opening the presentation to which you want to compare other versions of the presentations.

Did You Know?

If you do not want to apply all changes, then omit steps **7** and **8** above. Instead, use the Reviewing toolbar to review each change made to the presentation.

Preview It!

You can review changes made by individual reviewers instead of reviewing all reviewers' changes at one time. Before step **6** above, on the List tab in the Revisions Task Pane, click the Reviewers ☑, and then click the name of the reviewer for which you want to view changes.

Send your presentation as an
E-MAIL ATTACHMENT

You can send your presentation to others as an e-mail attachment. When you send a presentation as an e-mail attachment, your e-mail client opens with a new message with your presentation attached that is ready to address and then send.

By sending presentations as e-mail attachments, you can save time. Instead of finding a network location that all recipients have access to and then sending an e-mail message requesting updates to the presentation, you can instead just send the presentation via e-mail. When you send a

presentation as an attachment, you can look up recipients in your e-mail address book.

It also saves time to use Send To Mail Recipient as Attachment because it attaches the presentation to the e-mail message for you. Without Send To Mail Recipient as Attachment, you would have to open your e-mail client, start a new e-mail message, and attach the presentation to the message. These steps are taken care of when you use Send To Mail Recipient as Attachment.

1 Click File.

2 Click Send To.

3 Click Mail Recipient (as Attachment).

Your e-mail client opens with a new mail message created with the presentation attached.

4 Click To.

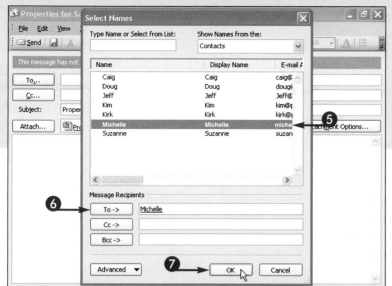

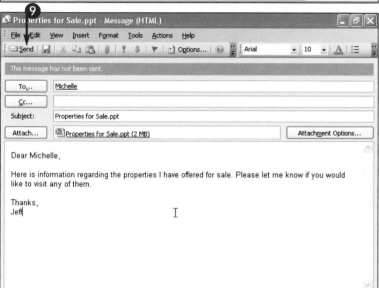

The Select Names dialog box appears.

⑤ In the Name section, click the name of those to whom you want to send the presentation.

Note: If you want to send to more than one person, press Ctrl+click to select more than one name.

⑥ Click To.

⑦ Click OK.

⑧ Type your message in the body of the e-mail message.

⑨ Click Send.

The message is sent with the presentation attached.

Caution!

You should use caution when you use e-mail to send large presentations. Some recipients may use e-mail providers that limit the size of attachments. Additionally, users with low bandwidth connections may not want to wait for large presentations to download when they check for e-mail.

Did You Know?

You can type the complete e-mail addresses of the people to whom you wish to send the e-mail message instead of looking them up in your address book. In step **4** above, type the e-mail addresses, separated by a semicolon, on the To line. You can then omit steps **5** to **7** above. If they are in your address book, their display names will appear.

Work together with
SEND AS SHARED ATTACHMENT

You can send presentations to others and ensure they are working with the latest version when you send presentations as shared attachments. Unlike presentations sent as regular attachments, shared attachments are stored on a central Web server running Windows Server 2003 with Windows SharePoint Services. Each shared attachment is stored on a separate Document Workspace, which you can think of as a small Web site that team members can use to collaborate on your presentation. Document Workspaces can include documents, links, lists of team members, tasks, and more. See Task #84 for more information on Document Workspaces.

When you send a presentation as a shared attachment, you specify the path to the Web server, and information about the Document Workspace is automatically inserted into a new e-mail message with a link to the Document Workspace. The presentation is also inserted into the e-mail message so that the recipient can work with the presentation even if one is not connected to the network. Once the presentation is sent, the Document Workspace is automatically created and a copy of the presentation is stored on it.

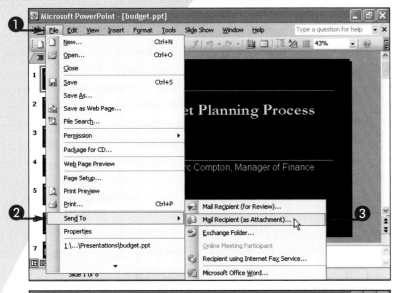

① Click File.

② Click Send To.

③ Click Mail Recipient (as Attachment).

Your e-mail client opens with a new mail message created with the presentation attached.

④ Type the desired text in the body of the e-mail message.

⑤ Click To.

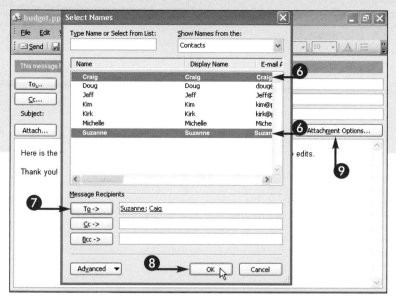

The Select Names dialog box appears.

⑥ In the Name section press Ctrl+click to select the names of those to whom you want to send the shared attachment.

⑦ Click To.

⑧ Click OK.

The Select Names dialog box closes.

⑨ Click Attachment Options.

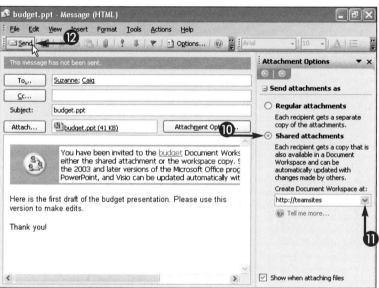

The Attachment Options Task Pane appears.

⑩ Click the Shared attachments option (○ changes to ◉).

⑪ Click the Create Document Workspace at field and type the URL of the Web site.

Note: For more on Document Workspaces, see Task #84.

⑫ Click Send.

The Document Workspace is provisioned, and the e-mail message is sent with the presentation attached.

TIPS

Attention!
Before you attempt this task, find out if your company has a Web server running Windows Server 2003 and Windows SharePoint Services. If it does, you need to ask the server administrator to grant you rights to create Document Workspaces. Upon granting you rights, the administrator will give you the URL to the server that you will need to perform step **11** above.

Try This!
Once you have sent a shared attachment, in step **11** above, a list of the familiar names of all the servers to which you have successfully connected to in the past appears. Click one of them instead of typing the URL in step **11**.

Open a
SHARED DOCUMENT
from an e-mail message

You can get the latest version of a presentation when it has been sent as a shared attachment. When you double-click a presentation that you have received as a shared attachment, you are prompted to check to see if there is a more recent version of the presentation on the Document Workspace. If you choose to get updates to the presentation, PowerPoint compares the version you are using with the version that is posted in the Document Workspace. If the version you are using is the most

current version, then the presentation simply opens. If the version you are using is not the most current version, you are asked if you want to instead open the more recent version from the server.

Once you make your edits to the presentation and save them, you are prompted to save your changes to the Document Workspace as a shared document. After you do so, anyone who opens the shared document is prompted to open your more recent version from the Document Workspace.

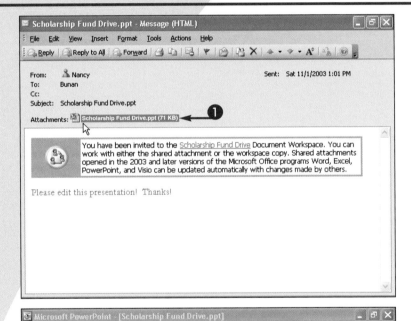

① Double-click the shared attachment.

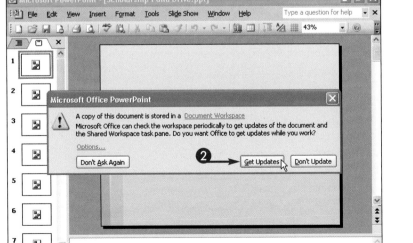

Note: If a dialog box appears asking if you want to open the attachment, click Open.

The Microsoft Office PowerPoint dialog box appears.

② Click Get Updates.

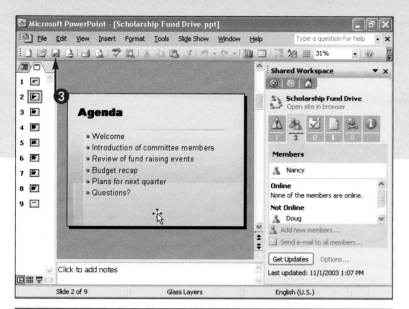

The most recent version of the presentation opens in PowerPoint, and the Shared Workspace Task Pane appears.

You can make edits to the presentation.

③ Click Save.

DIFFICULTY LEVEL

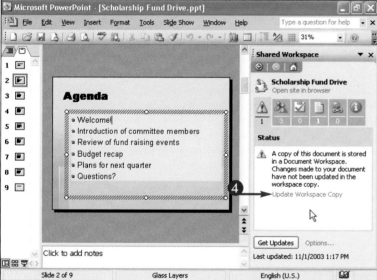

A notice appears in the Shared Workspace Task Pane asking if you want to update the presentation in the Shared Workspace.

④ Click Update Workspace Copy.

The presentation is updated in the Shared Workspace.

Attention!
The Status tab on the Shared Workspace Task Pane displays an alert when the version of the presentation with which you are working is no longer the most current. You can also click the Get Updates button on any tab to get a more recent version of the presentation.

Did You Know?
Changes made on the Shared Workspaces Task Pane are immediately updated on the Document Workspace Web site. Conversely, changes made on the Document Workspace Web site are immediately updated on the Shared Workspaces Task Pane.

More Options!
You can also use the Shared Workspace Task Pane to find out more about the presentation. Click the Members, Tasks, Documents, Links, and Document Information tabs to find out more.

Collaborate on presentations with a
DOCUMENT WORKSPACE

You can create a Document Workspace that team members can use for centralized storage and as a collaboration location. Document Workspaces are Web sites that are provisioned for you to store documents and document information, lists of links, lists of team members, and tasks. Document Workspaces rely on Windows Server 2003 and Windows SharePoint Services, and you must have access rights in order to create Shared Workspaces. Document Workspaces make it easy for you to work with others on your presentation because reviewers are assured that the presentations that they open are the most recent versions.

The Shared Workspaces Task Pane gives you a view of each Document Workspace without leaving PowerPoint to go to your browser. When you create a new Document Workspace from the Shared Workspaces Task Pane, it creates the Document Workspace on the server, and then includes a hyperlink to it in the Shared Workspaces Task Pane. You can add members, documents, tasks, and links to the Shared Workspace from the Shared Workspace Task Pane in PowerPoint or from the browser.

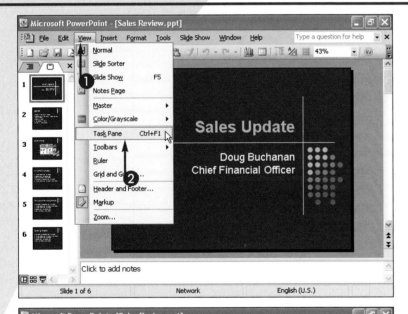

① Click View.

② Click Task Pane.

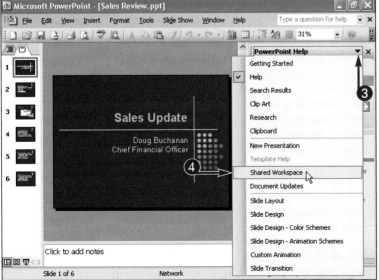

The PowerPoint Help Task Pane appears.

③ Click the Task Pane 🔽.

④ Click Shared Workspace.

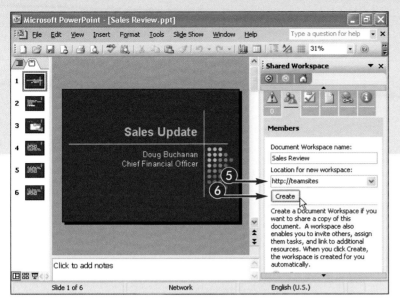

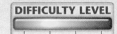

The Shared Workspace Task Pane appears.

5 Click the Location for new workspace field, and type the URL of the Web site for which you want to create the Document Workspace.

6 Click Create.

The Document Workspace is provisioned for you and reflected in the Shared Workspace Task Pane.

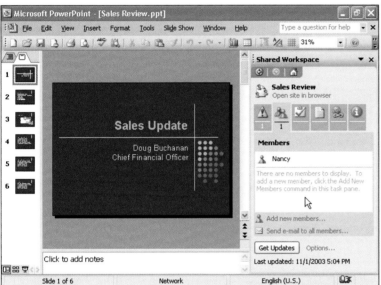

TIPS

More Options!
You can also make changes to your Document Workspace from the browser. To access the Document Workspace in the browser, click the Open site in browser link on the Shared Workspace Task Pane to open the Shared Workspace in the browser.

Try This!
When you create a Document Workspace from the Shared Workspace Task Pane, you are the only member added. By contrast, if you create a Document Workspace by sending a shared attachment, all recipients of the e-mail message are added.

Did You Know?
The filename is the default name given to a Document Workspace. For example, a presentation called budget.ppt would be saved to a Document Workspace at http://**<yoursite>**/budget/.

ADD RELATED DOCUMENTS
to a Document Workspace

You can use a Document Workspace to keep all related documents in one place. Document Workspaces are Web sites based on Windows Server 2003 and Windows SharePoint Services that are used to store related documents and lists of links, team members, tasks, and related information.

For example, if you have already created a presentation on budget plans for the next year and have stored it on a Document Workspace, you may also want to store a budget spreadsheet or policy document there as well. This allows all team members who currently have access to the

Document Workspace to also access the additional documents you upload. This can be much more convenient than creating a separate Document Workspace for every document with which you and your team work.

You can add documents to an existing Document Workspace by first opening the presentation that is already stored in the Document Workspace to which you want to add documents. When that presentation opens, the Shared Workspace Task Pane appears and displays the contents of the Document Workspace. You can then upload additional documents.

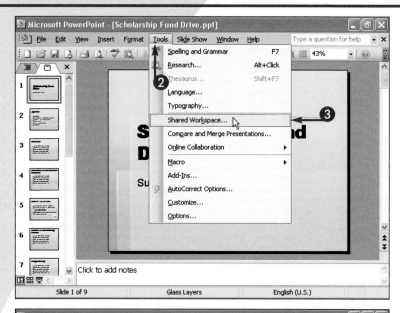

① Open the presentation that is stored in the Document Workspace to which you want to add a presentation.

② Click Tools.

③ Click Shared Workspace.

The Shared Workspace Task Pane appears.

④ Click the Documents button.

⑤ Click Add new document.

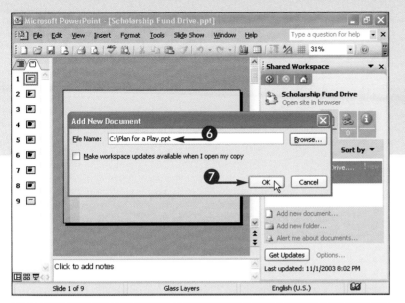

The Add New Document dialog box appears.

⑥ In the File Name field, type the path to the file that you want to upload to the Document Workspace.

⑦ Click OK.

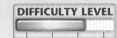

DIFFICULTY LEVEL

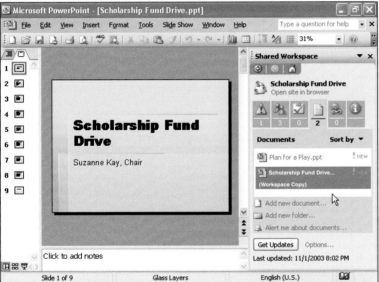

The presentation uploads to the Document Workspace.

TIPS

More Options!

You can also browse to a file to upload it instead of typing a path. Follow the steps above, but in step **6**, click the Browse button. The Choose file dialog box appears. Click the Look in ⬇ and then click the folder in which the file is located. Click the file you want to add to the Document Workspace, and then click Open. Then proceed with step **7**.

Did You Know?

Team members can also upload documents to the Document Workspace using their browsers. The easiest way to access it is to open a presentation that is stored in the Document Workspace, and then click the Open site in the browser link on the Shared Workspace Task Pane.

CHANGE TEAM MEMBERS
in a Document Workspace

You can change who has access to a Document Workspace in which your presentation is stored without leaving PowerPoint. Document Workspaces are Web sites based on Windows Server 2003 and Windows SharePoint Services that allow teams to store presentations, related links, lists, tasks, and related documents. Because each Document Workspace is a Web site, making sure that team members have access rights is essential.

When you add team members to a Document Workspace, they can be added by their user name,

Windows domain and user name, or by e-mail address. However, if you enter users by their e-mail address, they must also have a Windows account on the server running the Document Workspace.

Once you have added new team members to the Document Workspace, their names appear on the Members tab in the Shared Workspace Task Pane. You are also presented with a dialog box that asks if you want to send an e-mail message inviting new members to participate in the Document Workspace.

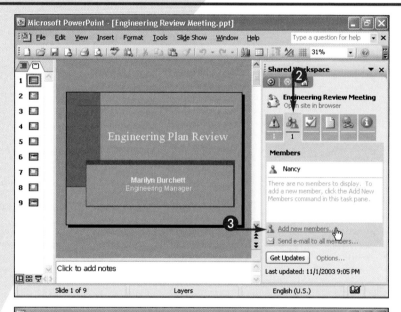

① Open the presentation that is stored in the Document Workspace to which you want to add new members.

Note: If asked if you want to get the latest version from the Document Workspace, click Get Updates.

② Click the Members button.

③ Click Add new members.

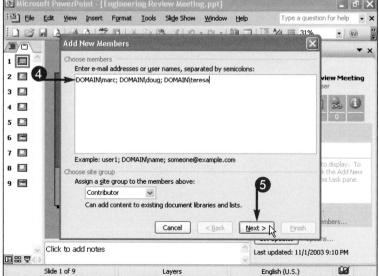

The Add New Members dialog box appears.

④ In the Enter e-mail addresses or user names field, type the e-mail addresses or Windows domain and user names.

Note: If you have multiple users to add, separate them with semicolons.

⑤ Click Next.

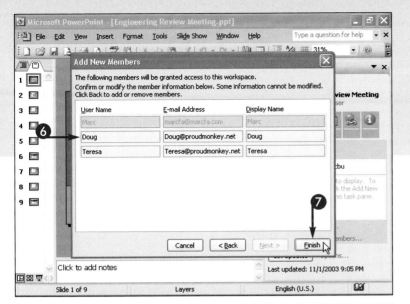

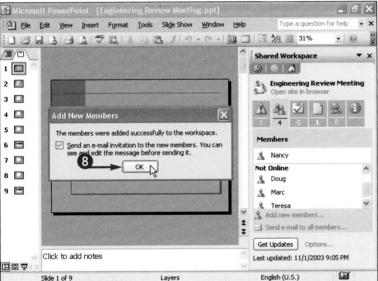

The next Add New Members dialog box appears.

⑥ Verify that the user names, e-mail addresses, and display names are the way you want them. If not, make desired changes.

Note: *This is your last chance to change this information before adding it to the Web site.*

⑦ Click Finish.

The next Add New Members dialog box appears.

⑧ Click OK.

New members are sent an e-mail message welcoming them to the Document Workspace, and they are listed in the Shared Workspace Task Pane.

Did You Know?

When you create a Document Workspace by sending a presentation as a shared attachment, all of the people to whom the e-mail message is addressed are added to the Document Workspace. When you create a Document Workspace from the Shared Workspace Task Pane, you are the only team member added.

Instant Message!

If team members are logged into instant messaging, and their instant messaging address is stored in your address book, the icons next to their names turn green, and you can initiate an instant messaging session with them. Log into Instant Messaging, click ▾ next to a team member's name, and then click Send Instant Message.

Track your
PRESENTATION HISTORY

When you save a presentation to a Document Workspace, version information is automatically saved with it, such as the dates on which it was saved, and by whom. Document Workspaces are Web sites that are enabled by Windows Server 2003 and Windows SharePoint Services. Document Workspaces allow you to save your presentation and related information in a centralized location for all team members to access.

Version history is especially useful when you are responsible for presentations that are being edited by multiple users. The ability to find out who modified each version of the presentation makes each team member accountable and helps give you confidence in delegating presentation work to others.

Version information is accessible from the Document Information tab on the Shared Workspace Task Pane. Each time a presentation is saved, a copy of that version is saved on the server, and information about that version is listed on the Versions dialog box. Version information displayed includes version number, date modified, by whom it was modified, the size, and comments. When multiple versions are listed, you can click any of the versions and then restore that version or even delete it.

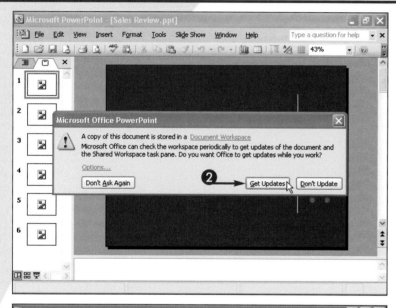

❶ Open the presentation of which you want to check the revision history.

The Microsoft Office PowerPoint dialog box appears.

❷ Click Get Updates.

The presentation opens with the Shared Workspace Task Pane opened.

❸ Click the Document Information button.

192

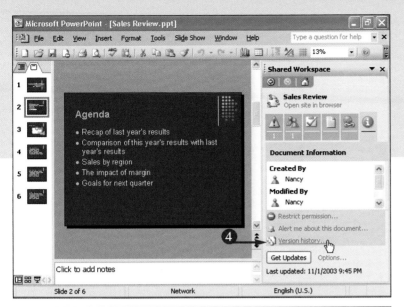

Document information appears in the Shared Workspace Task Pane.

④ Click Version history.

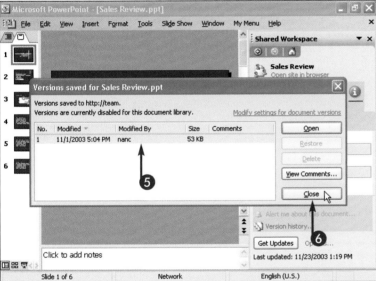

The Versions saved dialog box appears.

⑤ Click the version if you want to open that presentation.

⑥ Click Close.

TIPS

Caution!
Versioning is very useful if your documents are important and you need the ability to roll back a presentation to a previous version. However, because a copy of each version is saved every time the presentation is saved, it means that each version takes up more hard disk space on your server. Therefore, you might want to routinely delete versions that you no longer need to keep. You can delete unneeded versions by following steps **1** to **5** above, and then clicking Delete.

Caution!
When you delete a presentation, all versions of the presentation are deleted. Therefore, you should make sure that you do not need any backup versions of your presentations before you delete them.

Stay current when you
SUBSCRIBE TO ALERTS

You can stay updated on documents in your Document Workspace when you request alerts. Document Workspaces are Web sites that are enabled by Windows Server 2003 and Windows SharePoint Services for collaborating with team members on presentations. When you save presentations to Document Workspaces, team members can get the most current version of the presentation whenever needed.

However, when you are anxiously awaiting feedback from team members on a presentation, it is tempting to continually check the Document Workspace for

updates. Instead, you can request an alert, which is an e-mail message that is automatically generated from the server, telling you that your document has changed.

You can choose to receive an e-mail alert when anything changes in the Document Workspace. You can also specify how often you would like to receive alerts, such as weekly, daily, or directly after the Document Workspace changes. When you sign up for alerts, you are sent a confirmation e-mail message that contains a link to the Document Workspace, as well as a link to the alerts administration page.

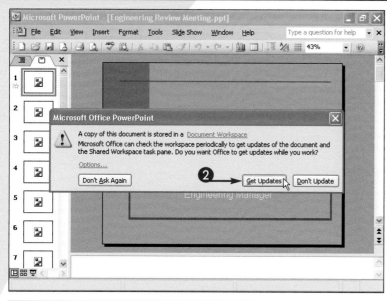

① Open the presentation from which you want to receive alerts.

The Microsoft Office PowerPoint dialog box appears.

② Click Get Updates.

The presentation opens with the Shared Workspace Task Pane opened.

③ Click the Document Information button.

④ Click the Alert me about this document link.

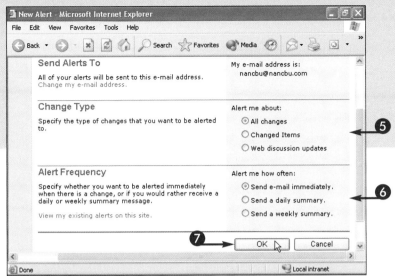

The browser opens to the New Alert page on the Document Workspace Web site.

⑤ Click the option for the type of changes to which you want to receive alerts (○ changes to ◉).

⑥ Click the option for the frequency in which you want to receive alerts (○ changes to ◉).

⑦ Click OK.

DIFFICULTY LEVEL

Your request for alerts is accepted, and you are automatically sent a confirmation e-mail message.

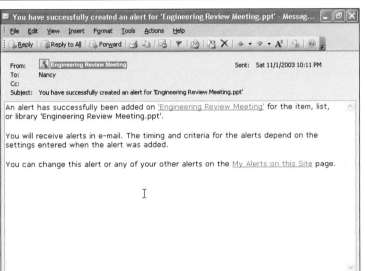

 TIPS

Save It!
The confirmation e-mail message you receive after signing up for alerts contains a link to the alerts administration page. This link is also sent in alert e-mail messages in case you want to change the frequency of alerts or even cancel your alerts subscription.

Caution!
When users are removed from the Document Workspace, their alerts subscriptions stay in effect. To protect the security and privacy of your Document Workspace, when you remove users you should also remove their alerts subscriptions.

Did You Know?
Document Workspaces that experience frequent use and continual updates may result in many e-mail alerts if you subscribe to receive them immediately. Busy sites with many updates may warrant daily updates instead.

ADD RELATED LINKS
to a Document Workspace

You can keep important information in one convenient location when you add related links to a Document Workspace. Document Workspaces, which are enabled by Windows Server 2003 and Windows SharePoint Services, allow you to save your presentation on a centralized Web server so that all team members can work with the latest version of your presentation.

Document Workspaces are displayed in PowerPoint on the Shared Workspace Task Pane. The Links tab, also displayed on the Shared Workspace Task Pane, allows you to add hyperlinks to direct Document Workspace

users to related Web sites and documents stored on your company's network.

For example, in a Document Workspace created for a presentation about new products, you could include hyperlinks to the product's marketing plan, to the product's Web site, and to a competitor's Web site, all from within the Shared Workspace Task Pane. Anything that you can link to from a browser can be linked to from the Shared Workspace Task Pane. When the visitor clicks one of the links, either the visitor's browser opens or the document or program linked to is launched.

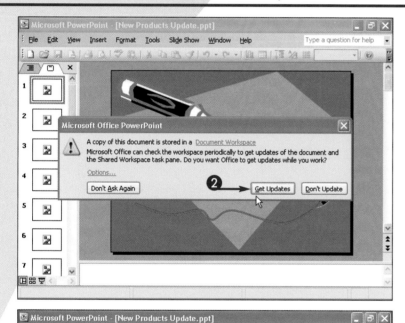

❶ Open the presentation in the Shared Workspace to which you want to add links.

The Microsoft Office PowerPoint dialog box appears.

❷ Click Get Updates.

The presentation opens with the Shared Workspace Task Pane opened.

❸ Click the Links button.

❹ Click Add new link.

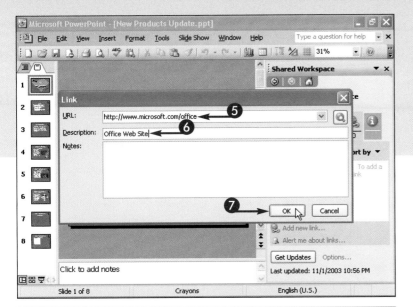

The Link dialog box appears.

⑤ In the URL field, type the URL for the hyperlink.

⑥ In the Description field, type the text you want to appear in the Links list.

⑦ Click OK.

89

DIFFICULTY LEVEL

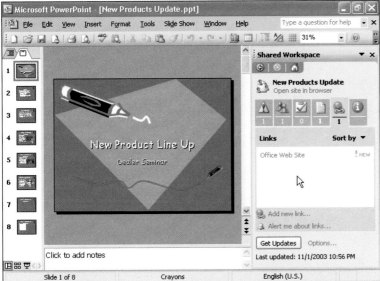

The hyperlink is added to the Links list.

Did You Know?

You can also browse to the Web site to which you wish to link if you do not know its URL. In step **5** above, click the Browse button (🔍) on the Link dialog box, and your browser opens. Browse to the Web page to which you want to link, and then return to PowerPoint. The URL is automatically inserted in the URL field. Proceed with step **6** to complete adding the link.

More Options!

You can choose to receive an e-mail alert when any of the links on the Shared Workspace Task Pane change. On the Links tab of the Shared Workspace Task Pane, click Alert me about links to sign up for alerts.

Deliver and Distribute Your Presentation Effectively

You can deliver effective presentations regardless of whether your audience is live or your presentations are available for off-line or unattended use. You can create a custom show that displays only a subset of the slides in a presentation. You can hide slides so that they do not display during presentation unless you specifically bring them up.

You can use Rehearse Timings to practice your presentation and determine how long it will take to present each slide. You can even program your presentation to replay after the last slide when you need to repeat a presentation.

If you have a Tablet PC, you can use your pen input device to draw on your Tablet PC screen

and display that ink directly on your slides. You can use NetMeeting to call an online meeting where your slides are on every participant's computer screen. As you advance your slides, the participants' slides advance at the same time.

You can create presentations for viewers to play in your absence by creating a kiosk presentation. Kiosk presentations play in Slide Show Mode and advance automatically to the next slide. You can also use broadcast capabilities to send your audio, video, and slides across your company's network for a true online experience. You can even burn your presentation to a CD and make it available for use by viewers who do not have PowerPoint.

Top 100

CREATE A CUSTOM SHOW
instead of a new presentation

You can create a custom slide show to save time and reduce the need to update multiple versions of slide shows. Custom slide shows are collections of slides in a presentation that you can play together. For example, if you have a large presentation that outlines your company's products and services, you may want to create a custom show that displays only slides about new products or a show that presents slides only about your company and its services. When it is time to deliver your presentation, you can choose the custom show to play in Slide Show Mode.

Without custom shows, you would probably have to create a different version of the presentation for each audience or for each use. This approach takes up more hard disk space and makes it difficult to perform updates because you have to find and then update each presentation. When you create custom shows, you keep all of the slides in the same presentation, which saves time and simplifies updating.

① Click Slide Show.

② Click Custom Shows.

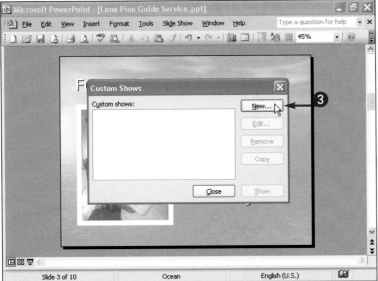

The Custom Shows dialog box appears.

③ Click New.

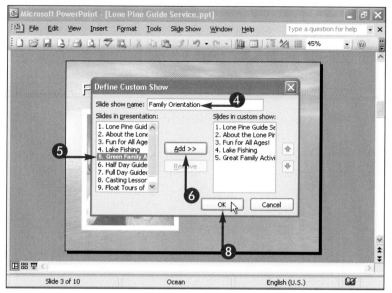

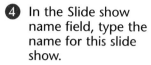

The Define Custom
Show dialog box
appears.

④ In the Slide show
name field, type the
name for this slide
show.

⑤ In the Slides in
presentation section,
click a slide that you
want to add to the
custom show.

⑥ Click Add to add the slide to your custom
show list.

⑦ Repeat steps **5** and **6** until your list
contains all the slides you want to include
in the custom show.

⑧ Click OK.

The Define Custom Show dialog box
closes, and the Custom Shows dialog box
is again visible.

⑨ Click Show to view your custom
presentation.

Your presentation plays in Slide Show
Mode with the slides you have chosen.

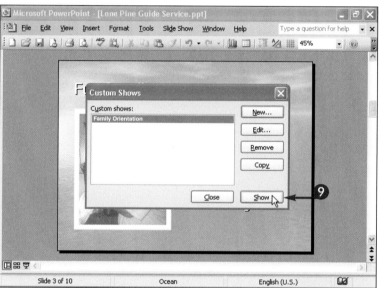

TIPS

Did You Know?
You can also create custom
shows as a way to reorder
slides for a given audience. For
example, if presentation time is
limited, you can create a custom
show that presents your most
important slides first in case you
run out of time.

Play It!
To play a custom show, click
Slide Show and then Custom
Shows. In the Custom Shows
dialog box, click the custom
show you want to play, and
then click Show.

Delete It!
You can easily delete custom
shows. Follow steps **1** and **2**
above, and then click the show
you want to delete in the
Custom Shows dialog box. Click
Remove and then click OK. The
custom show is deleted.

DISPLAY HIDDEN SLIDES
during a presentation

You can include slides in your presentation that do not print in handouts or display in presentations unless you specifically bring them up. These slides are called *hidden slides,* and they can be very useful when you have material that you may need to present, but are not sure.

For example, if you are presenting a complex or detailed subject, you may be uncertain how well audience members will respond to the material. You may wonder whether they will have additional questions or whether the basic material will be

enough for them. In this case, you can include slides in your presentation that are ready for use, but only if you deliberately go to them during your presentation. Similarly, you can use hidden slides when you have a time limit and are not sure whether you can complete all slides during a given time period.

Flagging slides as hidden is easy. When you give your presentation, the hidden slides are omitted unless you use Go To Slide to advance to a hidden slide.

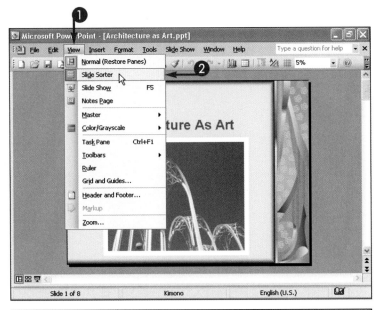

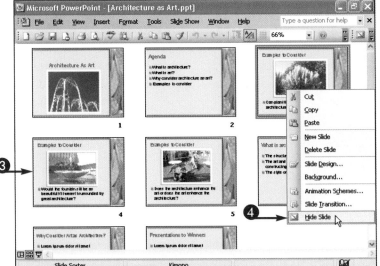

HIDE SLIDES

① Click View.

② Click Slide Sorter.

The presentation appears in Slide Sorter View.

③ Right-click the slide you want to hide.

The content menu appears.

④ Click Hide Slide.

⑤ Repeat steps **3** and **4** for all the slides you want to hide.

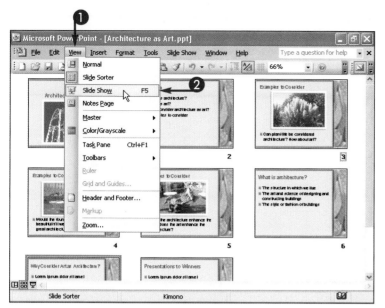

91

① Click View.

② Click Slide Show.

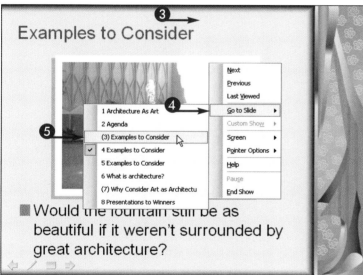

The presentation opens in Slide Show Mode.

③ Right-click the slide.

The content menu appears.

④ Click Go to Slide.

The list of slides appears.

⑤ Click the hidden slide you want to view.

The hidden slide opens.

TIPS

Did You Know?
When you use Go to Slide during a presentation, hidden slides are shown with the slide number in parentheses. For example, a non-hidden slide might appear as 2 Agenda, while a hidden slide might appear as (2) Agenda.

Attention!
Hidden slides appear in Slide Show Mode with a line through the slide number underneath each slide. The Slide Sorter is the fastest way to tell which slides are hidden.

Print It!
By default, hidden slides are not printed. If you want the slide to print, click File and then Print. In the Print dialog box, click the Print hidden slides option (☐ changes to ☑).

Practice your presentation with
REHEARSE TIMINGS

You can practice your presentation and record the amount of time each slide needs when you use Rehearse Timings. For example, if you are preparing to give a presentation where your time is limited, you can practice delivering your presentation so that you know whether you are spending too much time on one slide or not enough on another. Instead of using a stopwatch to manually record the timings, PowerPoint can do the work for you.

When you use Rehearse Timings, your presentation is displayed in Slide Show Mode, and the Rehearsal

toolbar is displayed. Every time you advance to the next slide, the time you spent on the previous slide is automatically recorded. Timings appear beneath each slide in Slide Sorter View.

Rehearse Timings is also a good way to assign times to slides that you use in unattended presentations. For example, if you create a kiosk presentation, slides in the presentation advance using the timings set when you use Rehearse Timings.

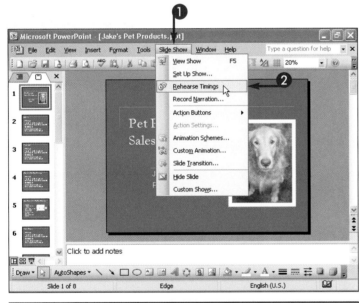

① Click Slide Show.

② Click Rehearse Timings.

The Rehearsal toolbar appears.

③ Click Next to advance to the next slide.

④ Repeat step **3** for all of the slides in your presentation.

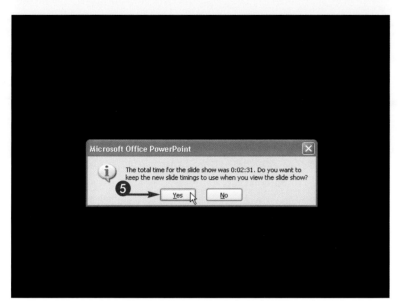

After the last slide in the presentation, the Microsoft Office PowerPoint dialog box appears, asking if you want to keep the slide timing for future use.

⑤ Click Yes.

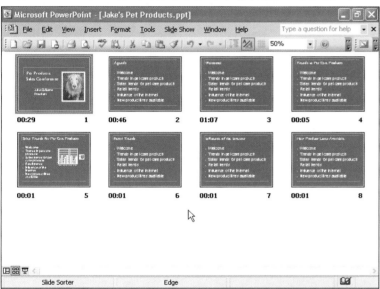

The presentation appears in Slide Sorter View with the slide timings noted under each slide.

Pause It!

If you are interrupted while rehearsing a presentation, you can click the Pause button ( ) on the Rehearsal toolbar. The timings stop until you click the Play button ( ).

Change It!

You can manually change slide timings for a slide. In Slide Sorter View, right-click the slide for which you want to change the timing, and then click Slide Transition. On the Slide Transition Task Pane, in the Advance Slide section, click the Automatically after option (□ changes to ☑). Click ▲ to select the number of seconds you want to use, and then click Slide Sorter View. The timing is changed.

Repeat your presentation with
CONTINUOUS LOOPS

You can set up your presentation to replay continuously by moving from the last slide back to the first slide in your presentation. This option is available by using Set Up Show to continually loop your presentation until you press the Esc key.

The ability to loop presentations is especially useful when you have to repeat a presentation without interruption between sessions. For example, if you have to deliver a presentation repeatedly in a booth at a trade show, looping the presentation saves time because you no longer have to stop and restart the presentation after every delivery.

Without the ability to continually loop the presentation, when you finish delivering your presentation in Slide Show Mode, the presentation goes back to Normal View in PowerPoint, which you would not want the audience to see, especially when your presentation is being projected onto a large screen. Instead, when you continually loop the presentation, you can advance from the last slide to the first without interruption because the presentation stays in Slide Show Mode the entire time.

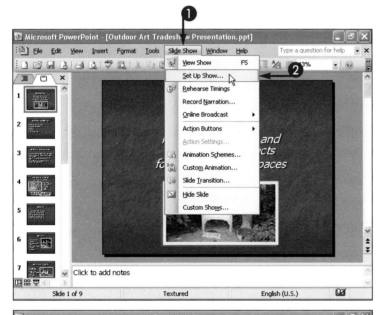

① Click Slide Show.

② Click Set Up Show.

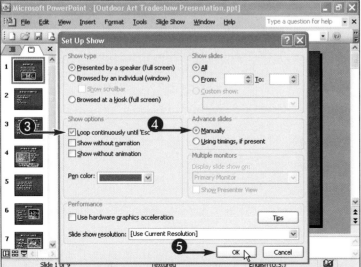

The Set Up Show dialog box appears.

③ In the Show options section, click the Loop continuously until 'Esc' option (☐ changes to ☑).

④ In the Advance slides section, click the Manually option (○ changes to ◉).

⑤ Click OK.

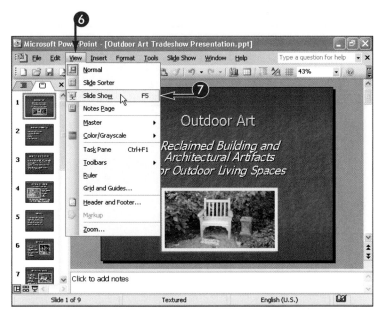

The slide show is set to repeat continuously until you press the Esc key.

6 Click View.

7 Click Slide Show.

The presentation plays continuously in Slide Show Mode. That is, after the last slide in the show appears, the first slide reappears, playing the presentation repeatedly without interruption.

TIPS

Did You Know?

You can choose to use slide timings instead of manually advancing each slide. Follow the steps above, but in step **4** click the Using timings, if present option (○ changes to ⊙) instead of the Manually option (⊙ changes to ○).

Did You Know?

You can create a presentation that loops only selected slides instead of all slides. Follow steps **1** to **4** above. In the Show slides area, click the From option (○ changes to ⊙). Click ⬍ to select the slide number to start with and the slide number to end with, and then proceed with step **5**.

ADD COMMENTS
during your presentations

If you are a Tablet PC computer user, you can use your pen input device to add free-form notes and annotations to your slides while you give a presentation. The Tablet PC pen input device allows you to draw on your computer screen, and your drawings are enhanced with colorful lines that look like they are part of the slides.

When you view your presentation in Slide Show Mode, you can tap the pen symbol with your pen input device to see the options available while

working with ink during your presentation. Options include changing pen type, which changes the width and shape of the ink displayed, and changing the color of the ink itself.

Once ink is turned on while you are in Slide Show Mode, you can draw freely on your computer screen, and those drawings are immediately visible to viewers. You can also change colors or pen type during your presentation if you want.

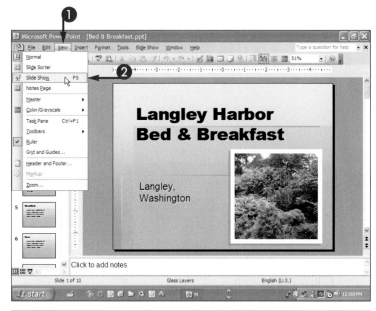

① Click View.

② Click Slide Show.

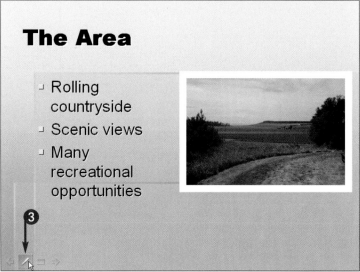

The presentation opens in Slide Show Mode.

③ With your pen input device, tap Pen.

The Pen symbol becomes visible.

4 Tap Pen again.

The content menu appears.

5 Tap Ink Color.

6 In the palette that appears, tap the ink color that you want to use.

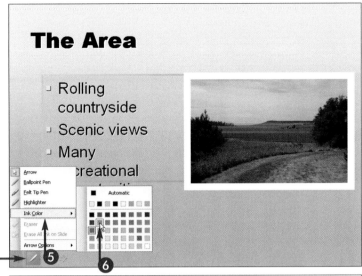

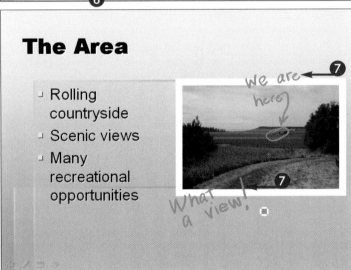

7 Proceed with your presentation, using ink to annotate the slides as desired.

TIPS

Try This!

You can choose the primary ink color for a presentation before you enter Slide Show Mode. Click Slide Show and then Set Up Show. In the Set Up Show dialog box, click the Pen Color ⊡, select the color you want to use, and then click OK.

Did You Know?

When you save ink with your slides, it is visible to all viewers of your presentation, including those who do not use a Tablet PC. It also prints on your slides by default.

More Options!

When you have finished delivering your presentation, you can save the ink with the slides or discard the ink on the slides.

Deliver your presentation in an
ONLINE MEETING

You can bring teams together when you schedule an online meeting, even if meeting participants are in different locations. Online meetings use Microsoft Office Outlook 2003 to schedule the meeting and Microsoft Windows NetMeeting to provide the online meeting capabilities.

When you schedule a meeting with Outlook 2003 and choose to flag it as an online meeting using NetMeeting, it automatically inserts server and connection information based on your existing NetMeeting configuration. Each participant who receives the e-mail invitation to participate in the

online meeting must also be able to access the server. For example, if the server you connect to is inside your company, participants outside your company may not be able to connect to it.

When the online meeting begins, each participant sees the same slide that you see. When you advance to the next slide, each participant sees that new slide as well. When you combine your online presentation with a conference call, you can discuss the slides as you give your presentation for a powerful online experience.

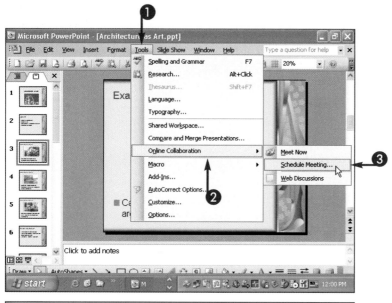

❶ Click Tools.

❷ Click Online Collaboration.

❸ Click Schedule Meeting.

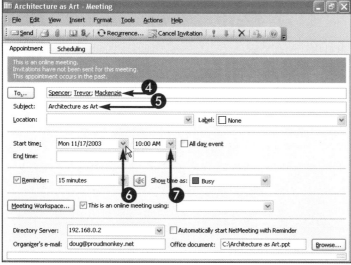

Outlook opens with a new meeting invitation linked to the document.

❹ In the To field, type the e-mail addresses of those you want to attend.

❺ In the Subject field, type the subject of the meeting.

❻ In the Start time field, click here and select the date of the meeting.

❼ In the Start time field, click here and select the start time of the meeting.

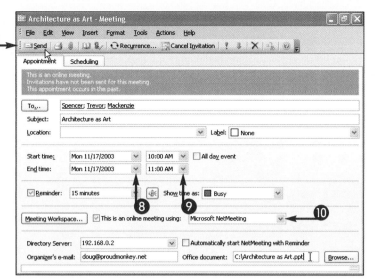

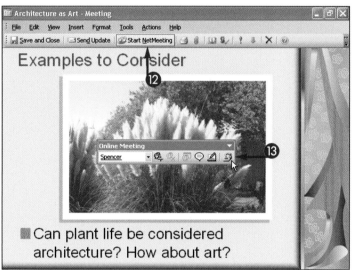

Examples to Consider

Can plant life be considered architecture? How about art?

DIFFICULTY LEVEL

⑧ In the End time field, click here and select the date of the meeting.

⑨ In the End time field, click here and select the stop time of the meeting.

⑩ Click here and select Microsoft NetMeeting.

⑪ Click Send.

E-mail messages are sent to each recipient.

⑫ Click Start NetMeeting.

The presentation opens in Slide Show Mode, and the Online Meeting toolbar appears.

⑬ Click the End Call button when the call is finished.

TIPS

Caution!
NetMeeting comes with the versions of Windows on which PowerPoint 2003 runs. To configure NetMeeting, click Start and then Run. In the Run dialog box, type **conf.exe** in the Open field and press Enter. When NetMeeting opens, click Tools and then Options. In the Options dialog box, click the General tab. Your system administrator can tell you the name of the Directory Server to which you should connect.

More Options!
During an online meeting, you can find out who is participating by clicking the Participants ☑ on the Online Meeting toolbar. This list is updated as participants enter or exit the meeting.

Did You Know?
You can add participants to the meeting from the Online Meeting toolbar. Click Add New Participants (🔲).

Create a
KIOSK PRESENTATION
that runs unattended

You can create a presentation that runs when unattended. Kiosk presentations play full screen in Slide Show Mode repeatedly until interrupted. Kiosk presentations are ideal when you want viewers to see your presentation but are not physically present to advance slides or restart the presentation when it is complete. For example, kiosk presentations are ideal for store windows and displays next to product merchandise.

Kiosk presentations rely on slide timings to determine when a slide should advance to the next

one. Slide timings are set by using Rehearse Timings, which allows you to rehearse your presentation and records the amount of time you spend on each slide. When your presentation plays, slides advance according to the times set when you rehearsed your presentation.

Once slide timings are set, the slide show is set up to display the presentation at the maximum screen size available and to use the slide timings. Once the presentation enters Slide Show Mode, it continues to play until the Esc key is pressed.

① Click Slide Show.

② Click Rehearse Timings.

The presentation opens in Slide Show Mode, and the Rehearsal toolbar appears.

③ Click Next when it is the right time to advance to the next slide.

④ Repeat step **3** until timings have been assigned to all the slides in the presentation.

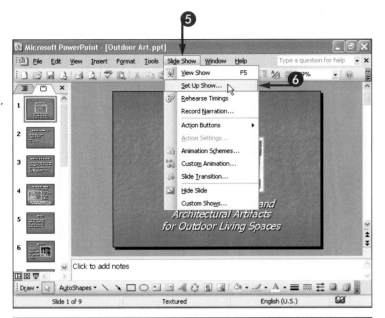

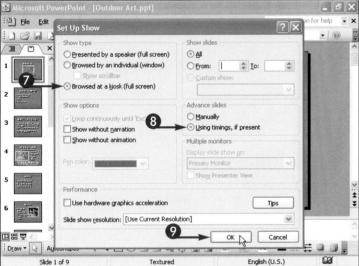

The presentation returns to Normal View.

⑤ Click Slide Show.

⑥ Click Set Up Show.

The Set Up Show dialog box appears.

⑦ In the Show type section, click the Browsed at a kiosk (full screen) option (○ changes to ◉).

⑧ In the Advance slides section, click the Use timings, if present option (○ changes to ◉).

⑨ Click OK.

The next time you enter Slide Show Mode, the presentation will advance automatically using the timings you set and will continually repeat after it is finished.

Did You Know?

Kiosk presentations work well with multimedia content. For example, presentations with slide transitions, audio, video, and animations can be more attention getting than plain presentations, and work well in kiosk mode.

Change It!

You can manually change slide timings for a slide. In Slide Sorter View, right-click the slide for which you want to change the timing, and then click Slide Transition. On the Slide Transition Task Pane, in the Advance Slide section, click the Automatically after option (☐ changes to ☑). Click ⬍ to select the number of seconds you want to use, and then click Slide Sorter View.

BROADCAST YOUR PRESENTATION
across a network

You can give a truly multimedia live broadcast presentation over your company's network. The Presentation Broadcast add-on for PowerPoint 2003 allows you to use your computer's microphone, and even use a video camera connected to it, to broadcast your slides, audio, and even video of you delivering your presentation to those who browse to a Web page.

Online Broadcasts use Windows Media technology to compress the audio and video to reduce the size of the presentation to send over the network. Using Online Broadcasts over your company's network is

recommended for ten or fewer users. For broadcasts with more than ten viewers, Windows Server 2003 with Windows Media Services is recommended.

When you set up a broadcast presentation, the default is to use audio only with the slides. As the presentation broadcast begins, you can deliver your presentation into a microphone while in Slide Show Mode, and advance slides as you normally would during a presentation. Participants can hear your audio and see your slides. As you advance your slides, the viewers also see the next slide.

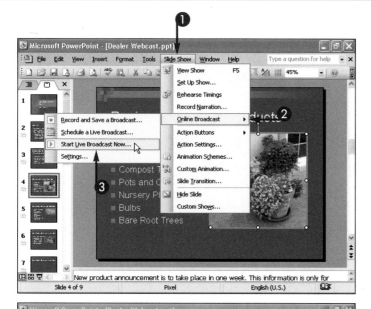

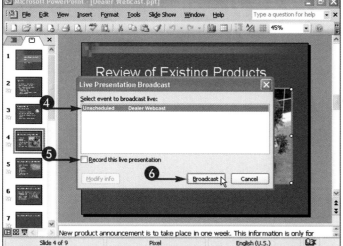

❶ Click Slide Show.

❷ Click Online Broadcast.

❸ Click Start Live Broadcast Now.

The Live Presentation Broadcast dialog box appears.

❹ Click the broadcast.

Note: Broadcast presentations you have given in the past are listed here as well.

❺ Click to uncheck the Record this live presentation option (☑ changes to ☐).

❻ Click Broadcast.

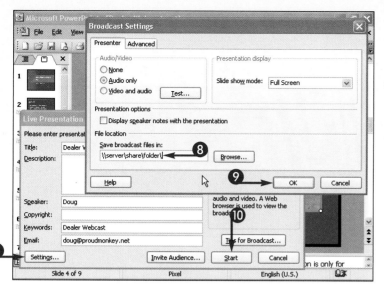

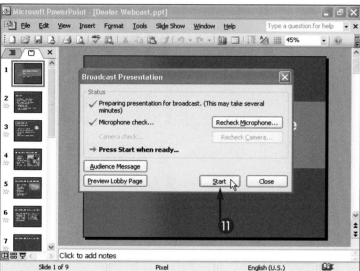

The Live Presentation Broadcast dialog box appears.

⑦ Click Settings.

The Broadcast Settings dialog box appears.

⑧ Type the network share path where you want to store the broadcast files.

⑨ Click OK.

The Broadcast Settings dialog box closes.

⑩ Click Start.

The Broadcast Presentation dialog box appears.

⑪ Click Start.

The presentation broadcast begins by opening the presentation in Slide Show Mode. As you give your presentation into a microphone, it is broadcast across your network.

TIPS

Check It Out!

The Presentation Broadcast add-on for PowerPoint 2003 is downloadable from the Microsoft Download Center at www.microsoft.com. After it is installed, the Online Broadcast option is available from the Slide Show menu.

More Options!

You can also display speaker notes with the presentation. In the Broadcast Settings dialog box, click the Display speaker notes with the presentation option (☐ changes to ☑).

Caution!

You must have access to a network share in which to store the presentation. Online broadcast files are stored in this location.

More Options!

You can use video as well as audio by clicking the Video and audio option (○ changes to ◉) in the Broadcast Settings dialog box, following step **8** above.

RECORD YOUR BROADCAST
to replay later

You can deliver your presentation online to allow participants to see your slides, hear your live audio, and even watch video of you delivering your presentation. You can even record your presentation for others to view later on demand from a centralized network location.

Record and Save a Broadcast saves the presentation as a synchronized multimedia slide show that includes your slides with corresponding audio and video if you used it. You can create this on-demand presentation by using Windows Media technology. When you expect more than ten users to view your

presentation at one time, it is recommended that you use Windows Server 2003 with Windows Media Services instead of playing the presentation from your company's network server.

While you are delivering your online broadcast, you can view the slides in Slide Show Mode, and speak into a microphone or a digital video camera with a microphone that is connected to your computer. As you advance your slides, the audio and video are synchronized to create a multimedia presentation that you can play back on demand.

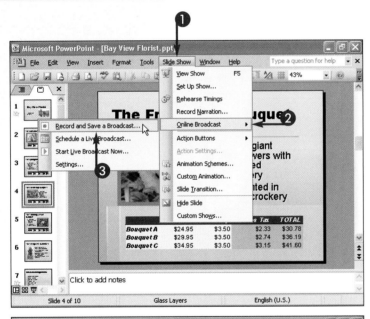

❶ Click Slide Show.

❷ Click Online Broadcast.

❸ Click Record and Save a Broadcast.

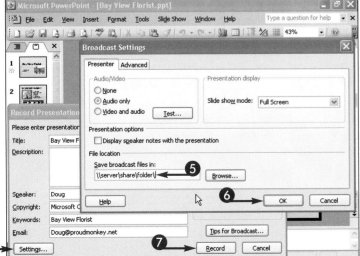

The Record Presentation Broadcast dialog box appears.

❹ Click Settings.

The Broadcast Settings dialog box appears.

❺ In the Save broadcast files in field, type the path to a server share to store the broadcast files.

❻ Click OK.

The Broadcast Settings dialog box closes.

❼ In the Record Presentation Broadcast dialog box, click Record.

216

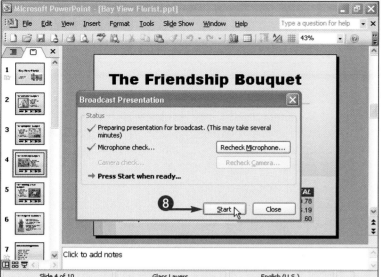

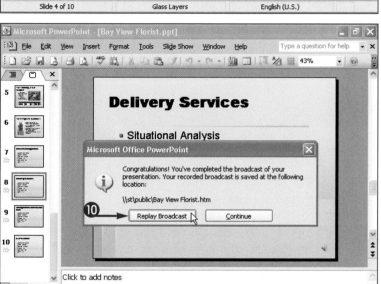

The Broadcast Presentation dialog box appears.

8 Click Start.

The presentation opens in Slide Show Mode.

DIFFICULTY LEVEL

9 Deliver your presentation in Slide Show Mode.

When you finish delivering your presentation, the Microsoft Office PowerPoint dialog box appears.

10 Click Replay Broadcast.

Your presentation broadcast plays in the browser.

TIPS

Caution!
Record and Save a Broadcast is available from the Slide Show menu after you install the Presentation Broadcast add-on for PowerPoint 2003. It is available for download from the Microsoft Download Center at www.Microsoft.com/downloads.

Attention!
When you finish recording your presentation, click the Replay Broadcast link to see the results. You should make a note of the path to the presentation so that you can invite others to view it.

Store It!
You must store the presentation on a network share, such as \\server\share\folder. The files created to run the multimedia presentation are also stored there.

Did You Know?
It takes more hard disk space and bandwidth to play videos. To conserve resources, use video only when necessary.

Play your presentation in
POWERPOINT VIEWER

You can make your presentation available to viewers even if they are not PowerPoint users by recommending the use of the PowerPoint 2003 Viewer. The PowerPoint 2003 Viewer is a program that is available free from the Microsoft Download Center.

For example, if you create a presentation about your products and want to distribute that presentation to your customers, you may be concerned about what to do if they do not have PowerPoint 2003. To assure that they can view your presentation, even if it is

password-protected, you can send them the PowerPoint Viewer along with your presentation. Recipients of your presentation simply open the PowerPoint 2003 Viewer, open your presentation, and it plays.

A convenient way to get the PowerPoint 2003 Viewer is to use Package for CD, but instead export the files to a folder from which you can copy the Viewer and the presentation. You can attach these files to an e-mail message or post them on a shared network for others to access.

① Click File.

② Click Package for CD.

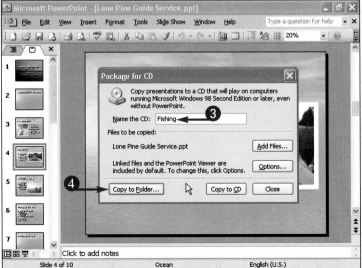

The Package for CD dialog box appears.

③ Type the name of the CD.

④ Click Copy to Folder.

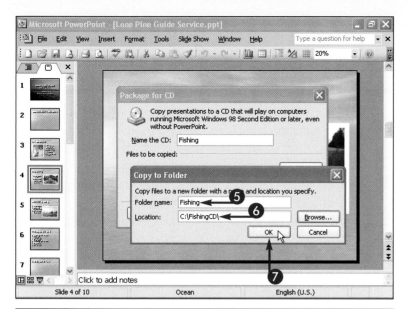

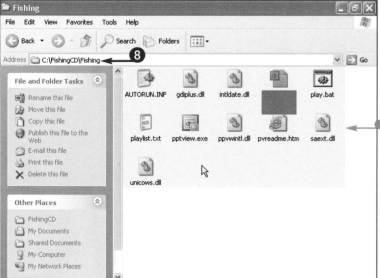

The Copy to Folder dialog box appears.

⑤ Type the name for the folder.

⑥ Type the path of the folder to which you want to copy your files.

⑦ Click OK.

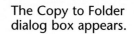
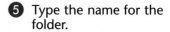
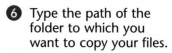

DIFFICULTY LEVEL

The files necessary to burn your presentation to CD, including the PowerPoint Viewer file, are created.

⑧ Open the Windows Explorer to the directory you specified in steps **6** and **7**.

● The PowerPoint Viewer and all of the files needed to view the presentation are available for distribution.

TIPS

Important!

The PowerPoint 2003 Viewer is designed for playing back presentations that have been created with PowerPoint 97 or later. Users of the PowerPoint Viewer 2003 can view presentations, but they cannot edit them.

Caution!

You cannot view presentations that use Information Rights Management or embedded macros, programs, or linked objects in the PowerPoint 2003 Viewer. Otherwise, even multimedia effects, transitions, and more work in the PowerPoint Viewer.

Did You Know?

The PowerPoint Viewer 2003 file is small, which makes it easy to distribute via e-mail. It is about 1.9 MB in size.

More Options!

You can distribute the PowerPoint 2003 Viewer with your presentations. When recipients open it, they must accept Microsoft's licensing terms before using it.

BURN A PRESENTATION CD
for a wider distribution

You can make your presentation available to a larger audience when you burn it to a CD and then distribute it. Package for CD makes it easy and automatic to package and then burn all of the files that are needed directly onto a CD.

Without Package for CD, you would need to create a new directory, save the PowerPoint Viewer to that directory, save your presentation there, and then have a developer create all of the files necessary to make the CD play automatically when it is inserted

into the recipient's CD drive. After that work is complete, you must burn the files to a CD.

PowerPoint 2003 simplifies the process. Assign a name to the CD, and then instruct PowerPoint to copy the files to the CD. PowerPoint communicates with your computer's CD burner to copy all of the necessary files along with your presentation onto the CD. When the recipient inserts the CD into his or her CD drive, it automatically opens the PowerPoint 2003 Viewer and plays the presentation.

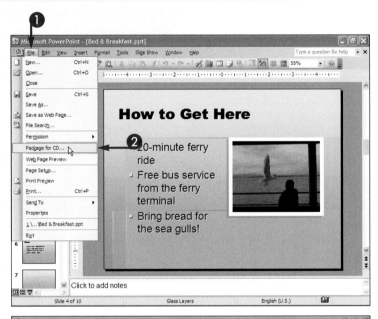

① Click File.

② Click Package for CD.

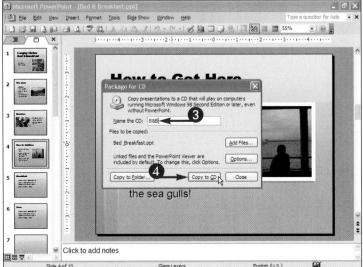

The Package for CD dialog box appears.

③ Type the name of the CD.

④ Click Copy to CD.

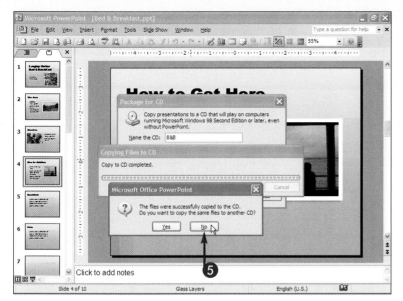

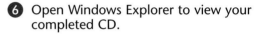

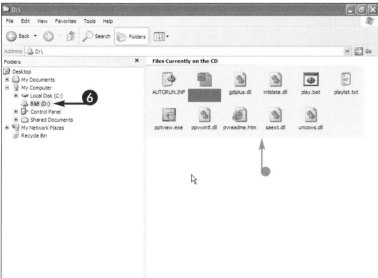

The Copying Files to CD dialog box appears, displaying a progress indicator on the status of your action. When the process completes, the Microsoft Office PowerPoint dialog box appears.

5 Click No.

6 Open Windows Explorer to view your completed CD.

● All the files you need for viewing the presentation are on the CD.

TIPS

More Options!
If you need to burn your presentation onto multiple CDs, in step **5** above, click Yes instead of No.

Try This!
You can add additional files to the CD if you want. For example, if you are creating a CD that contains a presentation about new products, you might want to also include a product brochure or price list. Follow steps **1** to **3** above, and then click Add Files on the Package for CD dialog box.

Did You Know?
In step **3** above, the name you assign to the CD is the name that appears next to the recipient's CD drive letter in Windows Explorer. Therefore, you should name your CD carefully.

Index

Numbers

3-D effects, 57

A

Action Buttons
benefits, 86
in button creation, 102
color, 113
create, 86–87
defined, 86, 112
test, 113
Action Settings dialog box, 87, 114
Add New Members dialog box, 190, 191
alerts
confirmation, 195
defined, 194
for link change, 197
receive options, 194
subscriptions, 194–195
alternative text
add, 158–159
defined, 158
as key words, 159
length, 159
preview, 159
Animation Schemes
apply, 99
categories, 98
defined, 98
for multimedia presentations, 121
select, 98
attachments
send presentation as, 180–181
shared, 182–183
size limit, 181
use benefits, 180
audio. *See also* **video**
add, 106–107
automatic play, 107
buttons, insert, 112–113
from CDs, 110–112
clips, insert, 106
fixed duration, 121
hover sounds, 114–115
looped, 108–109
narrated slide shows, 118–119
narrations, record, 116–117
in Normal View, 107
play, 107, 110
players, 113
sources, 100
symbol, 109
tracks, play selected parts of, 111
uses, 106
volume, 107, 109

AutoCorrect
for abbreviations, 62
defined, 62
enable languages with, 63
exceptions, specify, 63
uses, 58, 62
AutoFormat, 135
AutoShapes
3-D effects, 57
add text to, 56
colors, change, 141
defined, 56
in diagram creation, 122
enhance, 40
Format Painter and, 65
hyperlinks to, 124
maximum impact, 56
shadows, 57

B

background colors
coordination, 154
default, change, 155
photographs, 55
Background dialog box, 34, 37
background images. *See also* **images**
add, 34–35
apply, to presentation, 37
best, 36
digital pictures as, 36
graphic files as, 36
insert, 36–37
for Notes Masters, 37
print and, 34
stretch/contract, 34
texture, 35
width/height, 35
bookmarks, 84–85
borders
add, 46–47
dashed/dotted line, 47
defined, 46
line style, 47
line weights, 47
broadcast presentations
defined, 214
record, 216–217
setup, 214
slides, view, 216
speaker notes, 215
storage, 217
video/audio, 215
Broadcast Settings dialog box, 215, 216, 217
browsers
feature functioning and, 163
Microsoft Explorer, 162, 163
Netscape Navigator 3.0, 162, 163
optimize for, 162–163

Index

Index

Index

versions, 192–193
video. *See also* **audio**
    clips, play, 100
    embed, 104–105
    sources, 100
views, 4–5
Visual Basic Editor, 78–79
Visual Clarity Rules, 18–19
volume, audio, 107, 109

watermarks
    add, 22–23
    behind Handouts pages, 23
    defined, 22
    preview, 23
Web Options dialog box
    Browser tab, 163
    Fonts tab, 153
    Pictures tab, 161

Web Page Preview, 146, 147
Web pages
    hyperlinks to, 124–125
    link online presentation to, 164–165
    name, change, 149
    preview presentation as, 146–147
    save as, 148–149
    save presentation to, 144
    titles, change, 156–157
Web presentations. *See* **online presentations**
Web servers, 150–151
Windows Media Player
    control, 105
    launch, 102
    Object, insert, 104
    Object, size, 105
    Object properties, edit, 105
    in slide show, 104
words
    look up, 68–69
    translate, 70–71

Want more simplified tips and tricks?

Take a look at these

All designed for visual learners—just like you!

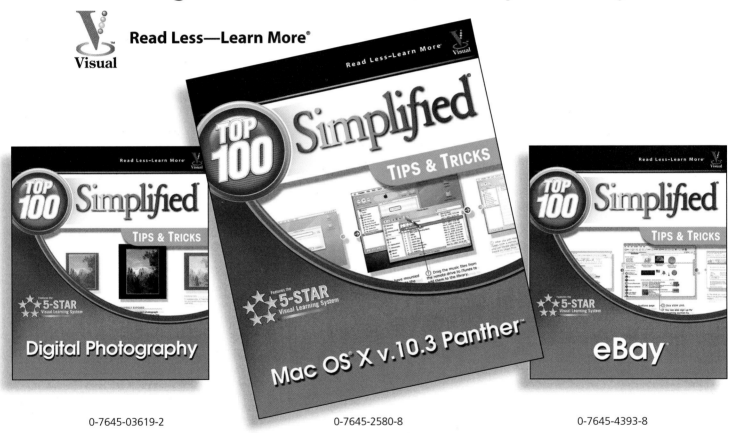